THE UNIFICATION OF GERMANY

MICHAEL GORMAN

Head of Humanities
Westfield Community School
Yeovil

CAMBRIDGE
UNIVERSITY PRESS

For my parents, to whom I owe so much

PUBLISHED BY THE PRESS SYNDICATE OF THE UNIVERSITY OF CAMBRIDGE
The Pitt Building, Trumpington Street, Cambridge CB2 1RP, United Kingdom

CAMBRIDGE UNIVERSITY PRESS
The Edinburgh Building, Cambridge CB2 2RU, United Kingdom
40 West 20th Street, New York, NY 10011–4211, USA
10 Stamford Road, Oakleigh, Melbourne 3166, Australia

First published 1989
Fifth printing 1998

Printed in the United Kingdom at the University Press, Cambridge

A catalogue record for this book is available from the British Library

ISBN 0 521 31730 4 paperback

Contents

Contents

Introduction

The declaration of the new German Empire on 18 January 1871 was undoubtedly the most important political event in the history of 19th-century Europe after the Napoleonic wars, thus making it a worthy subject for detailed study. Its impact in the years that follow was enormous. The focus of power in Europe was switched from Paris, where it had been located since the 18th century, to Berlin. Bismarck, the Chancellor of the new German Empire, had installed himself as the leading statesman in European affairs – historians often call the period 1802–90 the 'Age of Bismarck'. The humiliation of military defeat for Austria (in 1866) and France (in 1870) had important consequences: Austria became Austria–Hungary and turned her attention to the Balkans; France harboured an enduring enmity towards Germany. Both developments portended ill for the future.

Historians have identified many factors shaping German unification which are of great importance to the more general history of Europe in the 19th century. Foremost amongst these was the impact of industrialisation, which Germany experienced at an increasing pace after 1850. New factory processes led to a far greater range and enhanced quality of manufactured goods; transport improved, especially railways; new weapons and techniques could be deployed in warfare; vast amounts of wealth were generated. All of this greatly accelerated the process of unification.

In addition, the 1850s and 1860s witnessed the growing attraction of *liberalism* and *nationalism*. The chief beneficiaries of the economic developments were the middle classes, especially the entrepreneurs and financiers. They increasingly demanded that the nation of 'Germany' as an economic unit should be translated into political unification which, they believed, would lead to even greater economic prosperity. They also demanded a greater say in the running of the country; thus the traditional privileges of the aristocracy, accepted without question for so long, were challenged by an alternative ideology.

More than anything else, historians have pointed to the political genius of Otto von Bismarck, who played an essential role in manipulating internal and external forces which combined to unify Germany. His influence is crucial in explaining the events leading up to 1871.

It has been impossible within the scope of this book to examine all the factors leading to German unification. It has not been possible, for example, to analyse the influence of religion or the growth of a substantial working class on German unification. Further reading is essential and a guide is provided in the select bibliography at the end of the Introduction.

Commentary

The German Confederation 1815–48

Prior to Napoleon, the area on the map of Europe we now call Germany was a collection of over 350 small states and cities termed the Holy Roman Empire. Napoleon reduced this number to 39, and formed the Confederation of the Rhine to which 16 states belonged. This was to form the basis of the German Confederation (*Bund*), created by the Congress of Vienna in 1815 following his defeat.

Although there was a perceived sense of German unity in 1815, through language [1.1] and culture, many factors combined to prevent unification. While most Germans lived in central Europe, there were several isolated communities of German-speaking people in other countries, for example in the Balkans. Germans were divided by religion too. Broadly speaking, the 16th-century Reformation produced a Protestant north and a Catholic south and there were enduring hostilities between them. The German economy also did little to promote German unification. There were customs barriers on all routes [1.5] and no common currency or uniform system of weights and measures existed. There was not much political impetus to unity, either. The rulers of the separate states of the Confederation did not want to surrender their powers to a higher authority and the nobility sought to preserve their traditional privileges. The small but growing middle class consequently made little headway in obtaining greater political representation; agricultural labourers continued to fall victim to famine and plague, whilst those who sought security in the towns had to be content with appalling living conditions and the threat of unemployment.

It also suited the purpose of the Great Powers – France, Russia, Austria, Britain and Prussia – to keep Germany divided. After the defeat of Napoleon in 1815, the five major powers were of roughly equal strength in Europe, and consequently a 'balance of power' had been struck between them. A united Germany could upset this 'balance of power', a dominant notion in diplomatic thinking.

The Confederation was the creation of Prince Metternich, Foreign Minister and later Chancellor of Austria. He believed that any moves to unification would encourage nationalism in the multi-racial Austrian Empire and that a new national state in Europe would be a potential threat to Austria. He intended that the German Confederation should be dominated by the Habsburg Empire [1.13].

Prussia, the other Great Power directly involved in German affairs in this period, and the least of the five Great Powers in 1815, was prepared to work alongside Austria to contain the dangerous ideologies of nationalism and liberalism, spawned during the French occupation. This co-operation between the two countries was termed dualism.

Russia and Britain welcomed the Confederation for the same reason. France, which recovered rapidly after 1815, could hardly be expected to welcome the creation of a united Germany which could threaten her borders.

The very mechanics of the Confederation made unification impossible. The main governing organ was the *Diet* which met at Frankfurt. This was composed of ambassadors sent by the rulers of the member states; Austria permanently held the presidency. Provisions for representative constitutions in the member states and for improved trade were unevenly and unenthusiastically exploited.

Thus, the prospect of German unity seemed remote in the Confederation. However, there were two important developments which qualify this picture. First, the ideologies of liberalism and nationalism had developed in the middle classes. These ideas, largely generated by the experience of Napoleonic rule [1.3], were restricted to a very small group of people, and they permeated down to only a very few workers through small groups established in some cities. Initially liberal and nationalist activity consisted of passionate words but sometimes it was converted into action. Student societies called *Burschenschaften* were formed at sixteen universities after 1815 [1.4], beginning with the University of Jena.

These groups organised meetings to celebrate their patriotism; the Jena group had as their motto the words 'Honour, Freedom and Fatherland'. In 1818, fourteen of these groups formed themselves into the *Allgemeine Deutscher Burschenschaften.* A year later a member of the Jena Burschenschaften murdered Kotzebue, a playwright who augmented his income by writing an anti-liberal newsletter for the Tzar. This gave Metternich the excuse he had been looking for. He got the Diet to pass the Carlsbad Decrees [1.12], which imposed strict censorship on publications and close supervision of the universities and schools. The decrees were largely successful but did not stop occasional outbursts of nationalist fervour at later dates. The most important of these was in 1840 when France prepared to invade the Rhineland [1.5].

The second development was the formation of the *Zollverein* in 1834. This Union included eighteen states [1.8] and a population of 23 million.

The German Confederation 1815–48

Legend:
- Prussian Territories
- Habsburg Empire
- German Confederation

Scale:
200km / 100 miles

Labels on map:

RUSSIAN POLAND

East Prussia

West Prussia

Posen

Silesia

Pomerania

Brandenburg

Berlin

Prague

Bohemia

SAXONY

THURINGIAN STATES

Moravia

Vienna

Budapest

AUSTRIA HUNGARY

BAVARIA

Munich

WÜRTTEMBERG

BADEN

Frankfurt

NASSAU

Westphalia

Cologne

THE MECKLENBURGS

Hamburg

Bremen

HANOVER

HOLSTEIN

SCHLESWIG

DENMARK

NETHERLANDS

LUXEMBOURG

SWITZERLAND

KINGDOM OF SARDINIA

Venice

FRANCE

Paris

Germany 1867–71

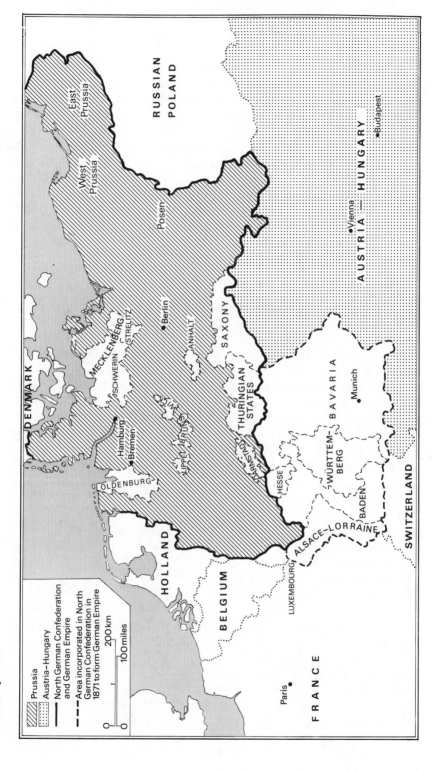

Prussia

Austria–Hungary

North German Confederation
and German Empire

Area incorporated in North
German Confederation in
1871 to form German Empire

0   100 miles
0   100   200 km

Austria was excluded. The Zollverein removed the economically crippling tariff barriers which had existed on the boundaries and even within the member states [1.7,1.8]. Although these had raised useful revenue for the rulers of the member states, they had been a massive disincentive to trade and had encouraged smuggling. Numerous German states now enjoyed considerable economic benefits from the new arrangement and it provided a powerful catalyst to economic development, notably in textile, iron, steel and coal production, and in the railways. Prussia gained politically too: railway construction centred on Berlin, and as Prussia negotiated for the Zollverein, she could threaten not to renew treaties if members dissented. The economic benefits were such that no member dared risk expulsion [1.14].

The revolution of 1848

The revolution of 1848 in Germany turned into an attempt by liberals and nationalists to unite Germany. The attempt failed. What were the causes of the revolution?

The German risings resulted from a combination of political unrest and social discontent. The middle classes were frustrated by their lack of progress: political power and senior posts in the army and the bureaucracy stayed firmly in the hands of the nobility. In the countryside conditions varied, but life for many became increasingly harsh. In the south and west of Germany, for example, the increasing population forced peasants to subdivide land. Rents were very high for those who had been emancipated, and all agricultural labourers were subject to the harsh impact of famine. Potato and cereal shortages also worsened the plight of the urban workers who lived and worked in appalling conditions. The craftsmen were particularly hard done by. The arrival of new technology and the drift of population into the towns undermined their business and caused overmanning which in turn led to poverty and unemployment. Revolts were by no means uncommon prior to 1848: a particularly serious outbreak occurred in 1844 amongst the weavers in Silesia, protesting at the decline of their industry in the face of competition from factories [2.1]. All these conditions intensified after 1846 through potato blight, drought, cholera and inflation; a depression in industry also occurred in 1846.

In February 1848 news of revolution in France sparked off demonstrations in German towns, starting with Mannheim in Baden, and then spreading north. Within days the bewildered regimes of the Confederation gave in to the demands of the revolutionaries for liberal reforms and constitutional change. Even Frederick William IV of Prussia was caught unawares. He initially tried to appease the rebels by making some concessions and by ordering his troops not to fire on them. This was not enough and the King capitulated even further, afraid of further bloodshed. The troops were withdrawn from Berlin, a liberal ministry was formed, and a proclamation was issued which stated that 'henceforth Prussia is merged in Germany' [2.7].

The most important development during 1848 was the attempt to unite Germany under a national assembly – the Frankfurt Parliament – which met between May 1848 and June 1849. Preparation had been made at the Pre-Parliament (*Vorparlament*) which decided that elections should be by universal male suffrage, although individual states had some latitude in defining exactly who should vote. Representatives were very largely from the middle class; there were only four craftsmen and one peasant. The Parliament was, in Carr's words, 'a galaxy of brilliant and talented personalities', yet it failed to bring a new Germany into being. It faltered over many issues. Throughout its existence the Assembly depended on the co-operation of the German states which were generally too overwhelmed to dissent. But once recovery got underway so the Assembly began to founder. Furthermore it had no money or armed forces to enforce its will. Its support for the Prussian repression of Poles in Posen, for example, drew charges of hypocrisy: successful revolution there would have diminished Germany, and thus it suited the liberal ministers to effect a *volte-face* from their previous support for national minorities. The Assembly's impotence was demonstrated over events in Schleswig–Holstein. In April it instructed Prussia to send troops into the duchies to protect the national claims of the German inhabitants. Foreign disapproval caused the Prussians to withdraw and sign an armistice despite the furious indignation of the delegates. The Assembly also spent far too long discussing the finer points of the Constitution: should Germany be a republic or a constitutional monarchy? Should Austria be included in the new Germany (*Grossdeutschland*) or not (*Kleindeutschland*) [2.8–2.10]? By the time it was felt that Austria should be included, the Habsburg government had recovered sufficient strength to frighten the delegates into effectively excluding her.

The liberals had gained temporary power largely on the backs of the rebellious artisans. Frustrated by the lack of progress, revolts broke out afresh in some parts of Germany in September 1848. The rebels demanded restrictions on new technology and a restoration of their economic position – demands that were anathema to the liberals. Once again, the Prussian and Austrian armies were called upon and thus the Assembly's impotence was again confirmed. The Crown of Kleindeutschland was offered to Frederick William IV on 3 April 1849. By then he was sufficiently strong to turn it down [2.11]. He did not want to accept it from what he considered an inferior class of people, and he proclaimed that he could not allow a written constitution to come between himself and his people. Furthermore, there would be a danger that Austria could resort to war and quickly stifle burgeoning Prussian hegemony in Germany.

The triumph of the conservatives portended much for the future. For the liberals, insurrection was clearly not the path to unification. It seemed that unification could only be achieved with the help of Prussia or Austria. North German liberals favoured Prussia, which already led in economic matters, and which did not have such a harsh record of political repression as Austria. The 1850s underlined this trend.

The years 1850–62

The 1850s are sometimes referred to as 'the quiet years' in German history, a time when Prussia apparently bowed to Austrian superiority. However, forces were at work which ensured that by the end of the decade Prussia was in the ascendant.

The 1850s certainly started badly for Prussia. It was clear after the revolution that a new arrangement to replace the Confederation was required. A Prussian plan in 1849 to dominate Germany in the Erfurt Union [3.1] failed through lack of support from other German states, and through the aggressive policies of the Austrian Chancellor Schwarzenberg, who forced Prussia to back down over armed intervention in Hesse-Kassel. Prussia and Austria now agreed to the Olmütz Punctuation (1850), which restored the old Confederation and hence Austrian supremacy within Germany.

However, the 1850s saw a decline in Austrian fortune. Attempts to link the Habsburg Empire with the Zollverein [3.2] were rejected by the major German states, under pressure from Prussia. There were no competent politicians to replace the able Schwarzenberg who died in 1852. And Austria's failure to help the Russians in the Crimean War (1853–56) lost her an important ally in German affairs. Numerous military campaigns, for example in Italy in 1859, incurred crippling expenses and few positive results. Austria continued to maintain her position within the Confederation but constantly refused to make any concessions to Prussia. In 1860, for example, the Emperor Francis Joseph refused to consider Austria sharing the presidency of the Diet with Prussia.

Prussia, on the other hand, was strengthening in many ways. In 1858 Frederick William IV's mental illness resulted in his brother William becoming Regent. He became King two years later. Like his predecessor, William believed that the monarchy had to be defended at all costs and Prussia must be upheld as the superior power in Germany. However, he was a more realistic man who understood the times better than his brother. The Prussian economy continued to grow too: for example, iron output rose from 0.5 million tonnes in 1852 to 1.29 million in 1857 [3.4]. And members of the Zollverein continued to derive considerable benefits from Prussian economic leadership too.

The late 1850s also saw a revival of German nationalism. Many had now come to realise that unification could be best achieved through Prussian leadership and in 1859 the *Nationalverein* was founded [3.3]. It called for the replacement of the Diet by a centralised government led by Prussia.

Liberalism also revived. In Prussia the *Progressive Party* made great headway with its anti-traditionalist policies. In March 1862 it held 136 seats in the *Landtag*, as opposed to the Conservatives' eleven. These revivals put pressure on the Prussian government to pursue policies aimed at enhancing Prussia's position in Germany.

However, liberals in Prussia were enjoying a false dawn; their aspirations were soon dashed by a serious constitutional crisis. The events preceding the Olmütz Punctuation, and the mobilisation against France in 1859, revealed the need for radical reform of the army. William I's Minister for War planned on doubling the size of the army and on reducing the role of the reserve army, the *Landwehr*. This was an odious suggestion to the liberals who viewed the Landwehr as a middle-class counter-balance to the *Junker*-dominated, aristocratic Prussian army. The argument dragged on for two years and in the summer of 1862, the Landtag, dominated by the liberals, refused any more money for the army. William I was infuriated that the Landtag was attempting to control the Crown's direction of the army, Prussia's most precious and necessary possession. He was faced with the prospect of abdication or the establishment of a military dictatorship which would in all probability lead to civil war. In desperation he sent for Otto von Bismarck-Schönhausen.

Bismarck and Germany 1862–66

Bismarck was associated with the far right in German politics, and his experience as Prussian ambassador in St Petersburg and Paris gave him considerable experience in foreign affairs. Beyond the immediate resolution of the constitutional crisis he aimed to elevate Prussia above Austria in the struggle to dominate Germany. Bismarck believed that Prussia deserved to play a far greater role in European affairs. He also sought to preserve the interests of his Junker class.

Whether Bismarck was a political genius is debatable, but he did inherit and exploit several favourable circumstances: the King often disapproved of Bismarck's policies yet dared not overtly antagonise or dismiss him as his own position would be threatened; the Prussian army had undergone major reform and was emerging as a highly trained professional force; the Prussian economy continued to boom and the positions of the other Great Powers in the 1860s were especially advantageous.

The constitutional crisis was resolved by what Bismarck claimed was a 'gap' in the constitution. He pointed out that there was no provision for the resolution of disputes between the two houses of the Prussian parliament, and that the decision consequently rested with the King [3.10]. He proceeded to collect taxes without the consent of the Landtag, declaring that 'the great questions of the day will not be decided by speeches and the resolution of majorities – that was the great mistake of 1848 and 1849 – but by iron and blood' [3.8]. His action prompted a predictably hostile reaction from the liberals, but their chagrin was short lived.

Bismarck was a great opportunist and constantly sought to exploit situations to his advantage. This was seen in the Schleswig-Holstein crisis which developed in 1863 and 1864. In 1863 the Danes attempted to incorporate Schleswig – a duchy which contained many German speakers – fully into the Kingdom of Denmark by approving a joint constitution. This infuriated nationalists and liberals in the German Confederation, and the Diet instructed armed intervention by Hanover, Saxony, Prussia and Austria. Bismarck did not want the Diet to gain any credit for success in the crisis, however, and so he decided to ignore the instruction and act with Austria alone [4.2]. Furthermore, he could not risk Austria posing as leader of the German nationalist cause as this would damage the progress made by Prussia since the 1850s. By posing as the upholder of international law he also obviated foreign intervention. The Danes were quickly defeated, and by the Treaty of Vienna all rights concerning the duchies were handed over to Prussia and Austria [4.3, 4.4].

Bismarck had demonstrated the impotence of the Diet and his willingness to break with convention to achieve his goal. There was immediate tension between Austria and Prussia regarding the administration of the duchies. This was temporarily resolved by the Treaty of Gastein which gave Holstein to Austria and Schleswig to Prussia. Bismarck now looked for the opportunity to completely exclude Austria from German affairs. He met Napoleon III at Biarritz in 1865 and made vague hints that France could have the west bank of the Rhine, which belonged to Prussia at that time, in compensation for Prussia's expansion in Germany, provided that France stayed neutral in any war between Prussia and Austria [4.6].

Relations between Prussia and Austria rapidly deteriorated after Gastein and in April 1866 Bismarck proposed to the Diet a new constitution excluding Austria and uniting Germany under Prussia. This infuriated Austria and terrified other German rulers and liberals. An international conference to avoid war was proposed but Austria refused to attend. She broke agreements with Prussia by referring the Schleswig-Holstein question to the Diet and this gave Bismarck the pretext he needed to occupy Holstein. Austria successfully mobilised the Confederation against Prussia, and Bismarck declared that the Confederation was now at an end.

The war that followed was over within six weeks. On 3 July 1866 the Prussians smashed the Austrian army at Sadowa in Bohemia, having overrun the opposing German states. Bismarck resisted King William and the generals who wanted to carry on further into Austria [4.7]. He did not want to make Austria irreconcilably hostile. In the Treaty of Prague of 1866 Austria ceded Holstein to Prussia and ceded Venetia to France, who passed it on to Italy. She also agreed 'to a new organisation in Germany without the participation of the Imperial Austrian state.' The German Confederation was abolished.

Prussia now replaced the old Confederation of 1815 with the North German Confederation, whose constitution ensured Prussian superiority and preserved the autocratic nature of government. Bismarck allowed the Lower House in the North German Confederation to be elected by universal male suffrage, a concession which delighted many liberals, but one which the Chancellor knew would benefit a monarch who provided material gains. Bismarck now enjoyed support from many liberals, especially in the North German Confederation [4.8]. As one liberal, von Schering, said: 'I bow before the genius of Bismarck. I have forgiven the man everything he has done up to now...' Bismarck also obtained an Indemnity Bill from the Prussian Landtag in September 1866 with little difficulty. This forgave the government for ruling without a constitutional budget since 1862.

There remained the problem of the southern states – Baden, Württemberg, Hesse–Darmstadt and Bavaria – now organised into their own vague union [4.9]. Bismarck probably wanted to include these states into Germany after 1866, but there was no clear way of doing this [4.10]. *Particularism* was a strong force in these few states, yet it was clear that the position of the southern states was only temporary. They still depended on Prussia economically (through the Zollverein) and militarily (through a series of military treaties signed in August 1866). Bismarck was also under domestic pressure to continue with unification. Furthermore, these States could be a threat to Prussia if they allied with another country, especially with France.

The Franco–Prussian War

Bismarck termed complete German unification as an 'unripe fruit' in 1869. War was the only means of generating sufficient national enthusiasm to secure unification, yet he was reluctant to resort to this uncertain path. France was now regarded as Germany's principal enemy. This was demonstrated by the furious nationalist reaction to France's claims on Luxemburg in 1867. Thus, without necessarily having either war or unification as a primary goal, Bismarck set about exploiting the crisis precipitated in 1870 by the vacancy of the Spanish throne [5.4]. The French government, riding high on a tide of anti-Prussian sentiment, was understandably alarmed when a Hohenzollern candidate and distant cousin of William I, Prince Leopold, was proposed for the vacancy. Gramont, the Foreign Minister, demanded his withdrawal. Leopold agreed but Gramont required Benedetti, the French ambassador in Prussia, to obtain further assurances from the King that the candidacy would not be revived. The King refused and told Bismarck so in the famous Ems Telegram. By editing the telegram Bismarck created the impression that the King had snubbed Benedetti. Five days later France declared war on Prussia [5.5, 5.6].

War between Prussia and France lasted from July 1870 to January 1871, although its most decisive moments came within the first two weeks. Bezaine, leader of the French armed forces, was beseiged at Metz. Napoleon III was defeated and forced to surrender at Sedan. A revolution followed in Paris and the newly-elected Republican government continued the war. Paris surrendered on 28 January. The harsh treaty of Frankfurt of 1871 ensured enduring hostility between France and Germany [5.9–5.13, 6.6].

Unification

The war provided the final impetus to unification. The southern states came under considerable pressure to abide by their military agreements of 1866; popular support for the war and tireless liberal campaigning for involvement made their rulers wary of refusal. After the war with Austria, France had demanded restoration of her borders of 1814 as compensation. Bismarck now made this information public, and by neglecting to point out that the demands were three years old, made it appear that France was seeking territorial expansion. Understandably, the southern states were alarmed. Yet the prospect of continued isolation seemed increasingly unrealistic: Prussian military and economic might would predominate in the long run.

Nevertheless the force of separatism remained strong in the south and Bismarck was obliged to make apparently major concessions, especially to Bavaria. For example, he had to agree that Bavaria chaired a Bundesrat Committee on foreign affairs and that she had separate representation at peace negotiations. But these concessions amounted to little in practical terms. In effect the new constitution 'Prussified' more than it 'Unified' Germany. The Emperor of the new Germany was always to be a Prussian, and was to appoint a Chancellor, answerable only to him. The new German Empire would have two representative assemblies: the *Bundesrat* (Upper House) and *Reichstag* (Lower House). The Chancellor would preside over the Upper House which comprised representatives of the German princes. This group had some political power, unlike the Lower House which, although chosen by universal male suffrage, could only delay laws [6.1–6.4].

The negotiations over, unification could now be proclaimed. Ludwig II of Bavaria was paid a substantial sum to ask William to become German Emperor. William now accepted the Crown from the princes, which his father had turned down in 1849 when it had been offered by civilians. In the Hall of Mirrors at Versailles on 18 January 1871 William was proclaimed 'German Emperor and King of Prussia'.

Key issues

Early German historians were fulsome in their praise for Bismarck. Heinrich von Sybel described Bismarck in 1894 as an 'incommensurable political genius ... who was a politician of great stock who sacrificed everything to the interests of the state'.[1] Erich Marks credited Bismarck in 1902 with having made Germans 'strong and manly'.[2] Few historians would today agree, although controversy continues over many issues. Nevertheless, there is broad agreement that Bismarck was a political genius who emerged at the same time as several fortuitous developments in German and European affairs. It is perhaps more instructive, therefore, to go along with Bismarck when he said that, 'man cannot create the current of events. He can only float with it and steer.' Let us now examine the historiography surrounding the key issues in German unification.

The state of European politics

Many historians have pointed to the 'diplomatic vacuum' of the 1860s which gave Bismarck an uncustomary amount of flexibility in promoting the growth of Prussian hegemony. As G. A. Mosse has written, 'If he played his hand with great skill, it was a good one in the first place'.[3] Austria, Prussia's rival in German affairs, declined in status in the 1850s from a position of dominance. The able Chancellor, Schwarzenberg, could not be adequately replaced after his death in 1852, and Austria's diplomacy suffered several major setbacks. Her failure to back Russia in the Crimean War, for example, lost her a valuable ally in the 1860s. Her poor economic record contrasted with Prussia's impressive success: Austrian coal production increased from 1.2 million tonnes in 1850 to 2.2 million in 1859, compared with 9.2 million to 14.7 million tonnes for the German Confederation in the same period [**3.4, 4.2–4.7**].

France, under the leadership of Napoleon III, found herself increasingly isolated in the 1860s. Her expansionist policies alarmed Britain, and her friendship with Italy, especially over Venetia, distanced her from Austria. Russia feared Bonapartism and was more inclined to support Prussia, especially after the Alvensleben Convention which enabled Russian troops to pursue Polish rebels over the Prussian border. Similar conditions prevailed immediately before the Franco–Prussian War in 1870. Austria felt no obligation to support France, having been let down in 1866; neither did Italy, whose desire to achieve full unification was thwarted by the continued presence of French troops protecting the Papacy in Rome. Thus the common interests of the Great Powers which had kept Germany divided for so long had virtually evaporated by the 1860s.

It should also be stressed that at the same time as Austria declined in her status as a Great Power, so Prussia grew. This was largely due to her economic strength which will be analysed below. Another factor of great importance, stressed by historians like G. A. Craig, was the reform of the army which got underway after 1859. The Prussian army was altogether better led, under the direction of Moltke, than the armies of Denmark, Austria or France. German war efforts were planned well in advance: in 1870 nearly 500,000 soldiers were rapidly deployed on the Western front during the Franco–Prussian War, whilst French reservists were still arriving from barracks. The Prussian army had ready-made iron bridges exactly the right size to cross rivers in exactly the right places. At Sadowa in 1866, the Austrians depended on a muzzle-loading rifle, the Lorenz. This had a much shorter range and fired fewer shots than Prussia's needle gun. Admittedly the French had a superior rifle, the chassepot, but in the War of 1870 the German artillery proved devastating on French cavalry charges [**5.11, 5.12**].

The economy

Over-concentration on political and diplomatic themes in explaining German unification has led many historians to look for explanations in the social and economic realm. Amongst the first of these was the British economist J. M. Keynes, who wrote in 1919 that, 'the German Empire was not founded on blood and iron, but on coal and iron.' This has been taken up by recent historians such as Helmut Böhme who have placed considerable stress on the role of economic developments. Böhme argues that these are of far greater importance than the events of 1864, 1866 and 1870.

The economic strength of Prussia and the German Confederation was undoubtedly of great significance in unification. Prussia was given a considerable boost by her acquisition of new territories, such as the mineral-rich Ruhr district in 1815. The Zollverein, formed in 1834, removed the numerous tariff barriers, and business boomed. Revenue to the member states increased considerably: in Bavaria for example, customs revenue was 2.1 million florins in 1831–32 but increased to 3.86 million by 1834.

The main stimulus to the economy came in the 1850s and 1860s, however. The length of railway track in Germany doubled between 1850 and 1860 and this gave a considerable boost to other industries, especially iron, steel and coal. Financial activity was greatly accelerated to facilitate all of this: in Prussia 67 joint stock companies were formed between 1825 and 1850; another 115 followed by 1858.[4] New banks were established, such as the Darmstadter Bank, and important financiers developed an interest in the activities of the State. The German historian Fritz Stern has shown how Bismarck benefited a great deal from the financial wizardry of the influential financier Gerson Bleichröder, whose activities helped finance the wars against Denmark, Austria and France. For example, the money in the State coffers increased from 4 million to 17 million *Thalers* when Bleichröder arranged the sale of the Prussian government's rights in the Cologne–Minden Railway.[5] Böhme demonstrates how Prussia prevented Austria from having any economic role at all in Germany, whilst constantly increasing her own.

There is, however, controversy over the political importance of the Zollverein. Certainly it largely excluded Austria from German affairs, and the revenues from custom duties frequently allowed Bismarck to by-pass the Landtag. Member states came to depend on Zollverein revenues, and Prussia was the dominant influence in the affairs of the Customs Union. But was it the 'mighty lever of German unification'? Some historians such as G. G. Windell think not. They point out that the member states did not abandon their political sovereignty or their hostility towards Prussia, and made this manifestly clear when they fought against Prussia in 1866. Böhme points out that the subsequent elections to the Zollparlament produced a very substantial number of particularist representatives. Thus it is not altogether accurate to portray the unification of 1871 as a formalisation of an economic reality which had been in existence ten years before. Other factors clearly need to be taken into account. Some historians also argue that the emphasis on the social and economic aspects of German history is distorting. It is most unhelpful, they argue, to treat the political and military development as being of limited significance.

Nevertheless, social and economic historians have managed to challenge many of the old accepted notions about German unification, and for this, Bruce Waller states, we should be grateful.

Liberalism and nationalism

Liberalism and nationalism can be traced back before the beginning of the 19th century in Germany. There were many different shades of liberalism, some more radical than others. What they had in common was a desire to end absolutism and institute representative government which would administer free speech, free press, equality before the law and religious toleration. The Napoleonic occupation gave encouragement to nationalism too. There is evidence of this in numerous speeches and writings calling for German national unity. Both ideologies were repressed by the Austrian Chancellor, Metternich, and it was not long before they became closely linked in Germany. For nationalists, unification could only come about through the removal of the individual state rulers and their props – bureaucracies, judiciaries, aristocracies and so on – and the establishment of a national government. For liberals these were the obstacles to representative government.

It used to be argued by some historians that these liberal and nationalist views were widespread in Germany, but more recent research has shown that they remained the preserve of the small urban professional class. Some ideas were taken up by small urban working-class groups, but generally liberalism and nationalism did not appeal all that widely. This was especially the case after 1848 when the liberal Parliament in Frankfurt had repressed workers' risings.

The 1848 revolution ended in failure for the liberals and nationalists and presented them with an acute dilemma: how could unification be achieved given the existing political system, but without violent revolution? They feared that revolution would unleash an uncontrollable uprising amongst the masses and provoke an equally devastating reaction from their governments and armies. Nationalism and liberalism went into decline in the 1850s but by the end of the decade they re-emerged with more realistic views on what was achievable.

The revolution of 1848 had also thrown up another problem: what was the best form of unification? There were those who advocated a 'greater Germany' (*Grossdeutschland*) which included Austria, and those who advocated a 'small Germany' (*Kleindeutschland*) which excluded her. North German liberals came to favour the latter on the grounds of Austria's record of political repression, the large number of non-Germans her inclusion would bring into a new Reich, and Prussian economic superiority. They pinned their hopes on Prussia achieving unification and in 1858 formed the *Nationalverein* to promote this end. Southern liberals, on the other hand, feared Prussian hegemony and formed a Reform Association promoting a *Grossdeutschland* solution. Nevertheless, the support of the northern liberals for Prussia was purely pragmatic: they still loathed the traditional privileges of the autocracy and the emphasis on an unbending loyal military. This is evidenced by the constitutional crisis of 1860–62 and their attitude towards Bismarck prior to 1866.

The victory over Austria in 1866 had an enormous impact on the liberals who, in the words of Otto Pflanze were 'anti-war and anti-Bismarck'.[6] Most were won over by his achievements, and although the liberal party became divided, Bismarck had no difficulty in passing the Indemnity Bill in 1866. This has led some historians to accuse the liberals of surrendering to Bismarck. Otto Pflanze has said that they were 'the victims of their own limited ends, their lack of genuine popular support and their lust for national power.'[6] Others have said that the ends justified the means and that their support for Bismarck was their most realistic chance of success. Other historians have analysed the constitutions of the North German Confederation of 1867 and of the German Empire in 1871 [6.4], and have arrived at widely differing interpretations. Some, like Luther Gall, have said it was a sensible compromise between liberals and Conservatives. Others have condemned it as thin veneer for absolutism. It certainly cannot be claimed that final unification was achieved on a wave of popular nationalist sentiment. Particularism remained strong in the southern states, and despite the enthusiasm generated by the war against France, their inclusion in the Empire was really more an acceptance of an inevitable reality on the part of the governments [6.1, 6.2].

Bismarck

Finally we come to the role played by Bismarck. Bismarck was highly intelligent, well-read, articulate and energetic. He was also neurotic, emotional, arrogant and had a gargantuan appetite for food, drink and cigars. He was without doubt the most important figure in 19th-century German political life and arguably the most important figure in Europe apart from Napoleon. His schemings, successes and failures have made him the focus for many an historical study, a number of which have been led astray by the myths which surround great leaders.

Bismarck, in fact, went a long way in creating many of the myths himself. Perhaps the most tenacious was the one concerning his plans in the 1860s. Bismarck liked to give the impression that from the start he had had carefully laid out plans which would secure Russian and French friendship so as to isolate Austria. Austria would then be cajoled into war with Prussia and once defeated would be out of the struggle for the domination of Germany. With the southern states now adrift, the way would be open for a Kleindeutsch solution which would be secured by defeating France in war. This view was taken up by many nationalist historians in Germany who were eager to portray Bismarck as a master planner. At the opposite extreme, A. J. P. Taylor, for example, has depicted Bismarck as going from day to day with no clear policy and merely acting on the spur of the moment.

Most historians have dismissed both extremes, but there remains ample scope for controversy. As we have already seen, Bismarck inherited many advantages and historians point out that he was greatly skilled in manipulating them. At the same time he was not a free agent. He was under considerable pressure from several quarters: his own Junker class feared the loss of their privileges to the burgeoning middle class, and liberalism was a political force Bismarck could not ignore. As T. S. Hamerow has argued, 'Bismarck's conclusion was that the established order must either become the instrument of nationalism, or be destroyed by it'.[7]

On the other hand, historians have pointed out that Bismarck did have clear aims when he arrived in office in 1862. His experiences in the Diet in the 1850s taught him that Prussia could only grow in Germany at Austria's expense and that Prussia's greatest strength was her economy. He also recognised that in excluding Austria from a Germany unified under Prussia he would attract support from the liberal–nationalist movement. This *realpolitik* also led him to what Otto Pflanze has called a 'strategy of alternatives'[6] in which he pursued a complex diplomacy designed to keep a number of options open until the last moment. This can be seen in many instances, for example in the problem of the southern states after 1866. A. J. P. Taylor has argued that Bismarck had no clear plans for the continuation of Prussian expansion after the defeat of Austria, but this is to underestimate the man. Other historians have pointed out that Bismarck did want to include the south, but was uncertain how. He therefore pursued several policies at once. He was prepared to resort to war, but only reluctantly, as it was an unreliable method which he could not fully control. He continued to tie the southern states closely to Prussia, for example, by a series of military agreements, and at the same time sought the opportunity to embarrass France, for example over Luxemburg in 1867. He understood the potential which a successfully-waged war had for stirring up patriotic enthusiasm, but although he was clearly implicated in the Hohenzollern Candidature Crisis from the start (as demonstrated by G. Bonnin) it is still not clear whether he really intended that war should be the outcome.

For some historians, like Erich Eyck, it was Bismarck's intention to unleash war on France: 'I personally feel convinced that Bismarck undertook it with the intention of putting Napoleon in a formidable dilemma: either to suffer a political defeat which would in the long run cost him his throne, or to wage war – and that he saw that Napoleon would prefer war.'[8] Others, like Gordon Craig, see Bismarck as really working to avoid war if possible: 'It cannot be said that Bismarck wanted a war in 1870, but, thanks to the crisis that he had encouraged, to Gramont's maladroitness in handling it and to the passions it released in French public opinion, that was what he got.'[9] A. J. P. Taylor has also argued that the inclusion of the southern states was not intended from the start but was necessary in order to continue the war successfully. But, as we have already seen, Bismarck intended to expand Prussia's interests at the expense of Austria from the 1850s. Thus it seems unlikely that Bismarck was operating without a coherent vision: unravelling his precise intentions at particular times is the key to his actions.

More broadly, some historians have seen the roots of 20th-century German aggression and of Hitlerism in Bismarck's actions. As Hans Kohn wrote, 'the Prussian victories of the 1860s and the transformation which they wrought in the minds of most Germans, laid the foundations for the defeats of 1918 and 1945.'[10] Others, especially Gerhard Ritter, have countered this by pointing out that Hitler's regime differed from Bismarck's in several important respects. For example, Hitler sought massive German territorial expansion, Bismarck did not; Nazism was an ideology attuned to the masses, Bismarck sought to preserve a conservative élite (though he did use the forces of liberalism and nationalism to achieve this).

Did Bismarck engineer German unification to serve his own ambition, as Otto Pflanze argues?[6] This point has been developed further by several left-wing historians, like Hans Ulrich Wehler, who argue that Bismarck's policies were symptomatic of an aristocratic élite striving to preserve its traditional privileges in the face of emergent middle and working classes. This was achieved through propaganda which created artificial fears of so-called state-enemies, oppression, and social imperialism involving the pursuit of a successful foreign policy which diverted attention away from domestic problems. In this Bismarck has been likened to Napoleon Bonaparte. Such themes, the argument goes, can be traced through German history to 1945.

Other historians such as Geoffrey Eley and R. J. Evans have criticised this view. They maintain it oversimplifies the very real constraints imposed on the élite by the middle and working classes, and overestimates the degree to which they could be manipulated. Bismarck, it is also argued, is portrayed in too poor a light. As Bruce Waller says, 'comparisons with Napoleon can only go so far ... there are essential differences: the emperor, not Bismarck, held ultimate power; the strength of parliament was considerable; freedom of speech and freedom of the press were marked; the law was sensible and respected ... and reckless as [Bismarck] was ... he had more than a Napoleonic degree of moderation.'[11]

The sources

The very wide range of historical interpretations outlined here makes it perfectly clear that examining German unification is by no means an easy matter. In 1976 it was estimated that over 6,000 books, pamphlets and articles had been written about Bismarck, many of which were written with vested interests. Weaving through the myths that surround Bismarck and finding a satisfactory position between those who see him as a demi-God and those who see him as irrelevant or evil, is a major difficulty: so too is standing outside our own prejudices. We must not judge Bismarck – we must explain him. The key to this is to balance Bismarck against the other factors which helped to bring about unification. The documents that follow are designed to help one to do this, and they have also been selected with the 'Key issues' discussed above principally in mind.

References

1 H. von Sybel, *Founding of the German Empire by William I 1889–94*, Mitchell, 1928
2 Quoted in G. P. Gooch, *The Study of Bismarck*, Studies in German History, London, 1948
3 G. A. Mosse, *The European Powers and the German Question*, 1958
4 E. Hobsbawm, *The Age of Revolution 1848–75*, 1975
5 F. Stern, *Gold and Iron: Bismarck, Bleichröder and the building of the German Empire*, 1977
6 O. Pflanze, *Bismarck and the Development of Germany*, 1963
7 T. S. Hamerow, *The Age of Bismarck*, 1973
8 E. Eyck, *Bismarck and the German Empire*, 1958
9 G. Craig, *Germany 1866–1945*, 1981
10 Quoted in B. Waller, *Bismarck*, 1985
11 Ibid.

Bibliography

There are many books on Bismarck and German unification. The best introductory accounts, written specifically for sixthformers, are:

I. Mitchell, *Bismarck and the Development of Germany*, Holmes McDougall, 1980

W. G. Shreeves, *Nation-making in nineteenth-century Europe*, Nelson, 1984

A. Stiles, *The Unification of Germany 1815–1890*, Edward Arnold, 1986

B. Waller, *Bismarck*, Historical Association, 1985

D. G. Williamson, *Bismarck and Germany 1862–1890*, Longman Seminar Studies, 1986

For more detailed study, the following selection of books are recommended:

D. Blackbourne and G. Eley, *The Peculiarities of German History : Bourgeois Society and Politics in 19th Century Germany*, Oxford, 1984 – an advanced study of major areas of controversy

H. Böhme, *An Introduction to the Social and Economic History of Germany*, Oxford, 1978 – stresses the economic roots of unification

W. Carr, *A history of Germany 1815–1945*, Edward Arnold, third edn, 1987 – an excellent book

G. Craig, *Germany 1866–1945*, OUP, 1981 – gives a more detailed study of the later period

E. Crankshaw, *Bismarck*, Macmillan, 1981 – a useful biography

T. S. Hamerow, *Restoration, Revolution, Reaction: Economics and Politics in Germany 1815–1871*, Princeton, 1958 – detailed, authoritative, yet very readable analysis

O. Pflanze, *Bismarck and the Development of Germany*, Princeton, 1963 – an excellent biography – very detailed

A. J. P. Taylor, *Bismarck: the Man and the Statesman*, New English Library, 1974 – interesting and provocative

Hans-Ulrich Wehler, *The German Empire 1871–1918*, Leamington Spa, 1985 – contains interesting perspectives relevant to the earlier period

D. G. Williamson, 'The Bismarck Debate', *History Today*, Sept. 1984 – a very useful article which summarises the historiographical issues

1 Forces of change and stability 1815–48

The unification of Germany was a remote prospect in 1815, even to those attracted by the idea. Germany certainly did not seem to pose a particular threat to the major signatories of the Treaty of Vienna, who left before signing the act dealing with the establishment of the German Confederation. Metternich had got his way; Austria was set to dominate the Confederation for the forseeable future. Yet there were economic and ideological forces at work which were to play a crucial role in the development of German unification.

The aim of this chapter is to examine the forces which sought to maintain the status quo on the one hand, and those which sought to induce change.

The German Confederation

1.1 German-speaking communities in Europe in 1800 (key below; map opposite)

(a) Predominant linguistic groups				
(b) Linguistic minorities		N		Norwegian
		P	p	Polish
		PR		Provençal
(a)	*(b)*	RR		Rhaeto–Romansch
BU	Bulgar	R		Romanian
CI	Circassian	RN		Ruthenian
C	c	Croat	RU		Russian
CZ	Czech	SB	sb	Serbian
DA	Danish	SK		Slovak
DU	Dutch	SE		Slovene
ES	Estonian	SO		Sorb
FL	Flemish	SW		Swedish
F	French	T	t	Turkish
G	g	German	U		Ukrainian
H	h	Hungarian	WR		White Russian
I	Italian		y	Yiddish
	la	Ladino			German Confederation
LI	Lithuanian			

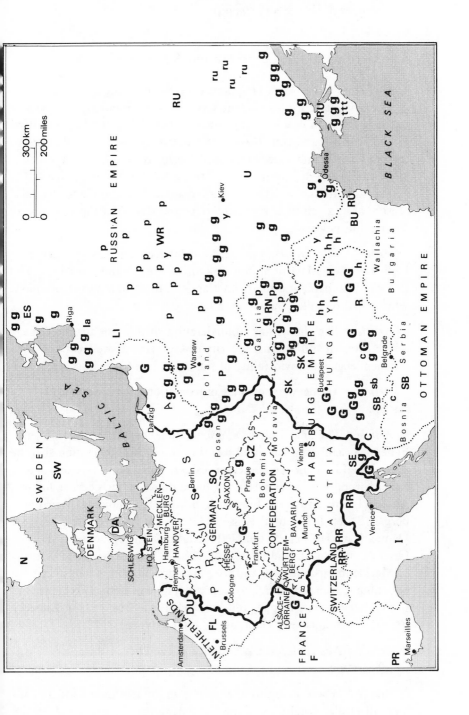

1.2   The German Act of Confederation, 8 June 1815

In the name of the Most Holy and Indivisible Trinity:

The sovereign princes and the free towns of Germany, motivated by their common desire to implement Article VI of the Peace of Paris [30 May 1814], and convinced of the advantages which would accrue for the security and independence of Germany and for the well-being and equilibrium of Europe from a strong and lasting union, have agreed to unite themselves in a perpetual confederation, and, for this reason, have given their representatives and envoys at the Congress of Vienna full powers ...

Article 1 The sovereign princes and the free towns of Germany, including their Majesties, the Emperor of Austria and the Kings of Prussia, Denmark, and the Netherlands ... unite in a perpetual union which shall be called the German Confederation.

Article 2 The aim of this Confederation shall be the maintenance of the external and internal security of Germany as well as the independence and inviolability of the individual German states.

Article 3 All members of the Confederation shall have equal rights ...

Article 4 The affairs of the Confederation shall be managed by a Federal Assembly in which all members of the Confederation shall be represented by their plenipotentiaries, who shall each have one vote either severally, or as representing more than one member, as follows; Austria 1 vote, Prussia 1, Bavaria 1, Saxony 1, Hanover 1, Württemberg 1, Baden 1, Electoral Hesse 1, Grand Duchy of Hesse 1, Denmark for Holstein 1, the Netherlands for Luxembourg 1, the Grand Ducal and Ducal Houses of Saxony 1, Brunswick and Nassau 1, Mecklenburg-Schwerin and Mecklenburg–Strelitz 1, Holstein–Oldenburg, Anhalt and Schwarzburg 1, Hohenzollern, Leichtenstein, Reuss, Schaumburg-Lippe, and Waldeck 1, the free cities of Lübeck, Frankfurt, Bremen and Hamburg 1; total 17 votes.

Article 5 Austria has the presidence in the Diet of the Confederation ...

Article 6 When these proposals relate to the enactment and amendment of fundamental laws of the Confederation ... the Federal Assembly forms itself into a plenary session, in which the component

members shall have the following votes proportioned to the extent of
their territories:

Austria, Prussia, Saxony, Bavaria, Hanover and Württemberg, 4
votes each, Baden, Electoral Hesse, Grand Duchy of Hesse, Holstein
and Luxembourg, 3 votes each; Brunswick, Mecklenburg–Schwerin   40
and Nassau, 2 votes each; (other minor states and free cities) 1 vote
each; total 69 votes ...

Article 7 The Federal Assembly decides by simple majority what
proposals should be submitted to a plenary session. The proposals
which are to be submitted to a plenary session are to be prepared by   45
the Federal Assembly ... decisions in both bodies are taken by majority vote, simple in the case of the Federal Assembly, two thirds in the
plenary session. In the Federal Assembly the president has a casting
vote. In matters relating to the enactment or amendment of fundamental laws, to organic federal institutions, to individual rights, or   50
religious affairs, unanimity is required in both assemblies ...

Article 11 All members of the Confederation pledge themselves to
protect Germany as a whole ... If war is declared by the Confederation, no individual member may negotiate separately with the
enemy, conclude an armistice, or make peace.   55

Article 12 The members of the Confederation reserve the right to
themselves of forming alliances of any kind. However, they pledge
themselves to make no commitments that shall be directed against the
security of the Confederation or any individual state within it.

Article 13 In all Confederate states there will be a constitution   60
providing for representation by estates ...

Article 19 The members of the Confederation also engage, on the
first meeting of the Diet, to take into consideration the state of
commerce and intercourse between the states of the Confederation, as
well as that of navigation, on the principles adopted by the Congress   65
of Vienna ...

Annual Register, 1815, in L. Snyder, *Documents of German History*, New
York, 1958

Questions

1   Study the language map of Europe [1.1].
    (i)   What is the predominant language spoken in the German
          Confederation?
    (ii) What other languages are spoken in the German Confederation?
    (iii) What are the predominent languages spoken in the Austrian
          Empire?
    (iv) In which areas outside the Confederation and Austrian Empire is
          German spoken?
2   In what ways do you think language was an important factor in:
    (i) promoting and (ii) preventing German unification? Account for
    your answer.
3   Explain what is meant by: (i) Federal Assembly [1.2, line 20]
    (ii) plenary session [line 35] (iii) organic federal institution [line 50]
    (iv) representation by estates [line 61].
4   What does the first line of the Act [1.2] tell you about the attitude of
    the signatories to the nature of their authority? Explain.
5   What parts of the Act [1.2] facilitated Austrian domination of the
    Confederation? Explain.
6   Which sections of the Act do you think would be pleasing to:
    (i) German princes?
    (ii) German liberals?
    Explain your choices.
7   'The German settlement of 1815 was part of a European settlement:
    it was drawn up partly in the interests of the German princes, largely
    in the interests of the great powers, and not at all in the interests of
    the German people.' Discuss.

Liberalism and nationalism

The French occupation of the Rhineland, from 1792 to 1814, was just
one of several factors which led to an increase in nationalism and
liberalism in the German states. The two ideologies became closely
linked. Look at the following documents carefully. The first is by Johann
Fichte, a philosopher whose *Addresses to the German Nation* earned him a
place as the first rector of the newly founded University of Berlin. The
second is by Karl von Hase, a founder member of the Burschenschaften.

1.3   Nationalism: Johann Fichte writes on German liberty in *Addresses to the German Nation*, 1807–8

Our earliest common ancestors, the primordial stock of the new culture, the Germans, as the Romans called them, courageously resisted the world domination of the Romans. Did the Germans not recognise the superior brilliance of the nearby Roman provinces and the more refined enjoyments in these provinces, as well as the abun-   5
dance of laws, judge's seats, lictor's axes and rods? ...

The decendants [of these Germans], as soon as they could do so without losing their freedom, even went so far as to assimilate the Roman culture, insofar as this was possible without losing their identity. Let us ask why, then, did they struggle for several gene-   10
rations in sanguinary conflicts that broke out again and again with greater and greater force? A Roman writer places these words into the mouths of their leaders: 'What was there left for them to do, except to maintain their liberty or perish before they became slaves?' Liberty to them meant this: persisting to remain Germans and continuing the   15
task of settling their own problems, independently and in consonance with the original spirit of their race ... and propagating this indepen-
dence in their posterity ... They assumed as a matter of course that every German would rather die than become Roman ... We, the inheritors of their soil, their language and their way of thinking, must   20
thank them for being Germans ...

Our present problem ... is simply to preserve the existence and continuity of what is German. All other differences vanish before this higher point of view ... It is essential that the higher love of Fatherland, for the entire people of the German nation, reign supreme, and   25
justly so, in every particular German state. No one of them can lose sight of the higher interest without alienating everything that is noble and good ...

Johann Gottlieb Fichte, *Werke*, ed. Fritz Medicus, 1807–8, pp. 365–611 passim

1.4   Liberalism: a speech by Karl von Hase, a nineteen year-old student, on 18 October 1820, to the Youth of the Free Universities of Germany, commemorating the battle of Leipzig

A people who fought seven years ago on this battlefield is worthy of a better fate. And if the magnificence of the great day has disappeared, if all the palms of victory have withered, if all the medals and trophies of great victories have faded, if all hopes have been deceived – one thing remains and shall remain, that is the visions proclaimed on that day ...

The first vision seems to me to be this: happiness and pleasure are not the highest aims of the people, but freedom. That is the will of God and reason.

From this it follows: the happiness and the greatness of a people depend only on the highest possible liberty of all citizens and the equality of all, established by laws they make themselves or that are made by their representatives.

The third, however, is a heart-stirring conviction which is instinctive in every truly great person. An enthusiastic people which is willing to fight for such laws and for such a Fatherland cannot be conquered – even if there are one hundred thousand Persians standing against ten thousand heroes of Marathon ...

The fourth belongs to us alone and is the most beautiful of all: Germans are we all together! There are few Saxons, few Bavarians, no more Hessians; the Franks do not wish to say much, the Prussians can be mastered; but that wonderful people from the Weichsel to the Vosges, from the North Sea over the Alps to Carpathia, made equal through speech, customs, and descent, all citizens of the Reich – a unified people of brothers is irresistible ...

You, ghosts of the fallen, be our witnesses, ghosts of our great fathers, look upon us! We swear never to flinch, never to tremble, we swear in this dark hour our loyalty to the Fatherland, loyalty to all good and beautiful, loyalty until death ...

Karl von Hase, *Reden und die Jünglinge der freien Hochschulen Deutsch-lands,* in Theodor Flathe, ed., *Deutsche Reden: Denkmäler zur vater-ländischen Geschichte des neunzehnten Jahrhunderts,* Leipzig, 1893, vol. i, pp. 88–103

French flag: 'We don't ever want to have the old German Rhine.'

German flag: 'They shall never have the old German Rhine.'

France

Don't sing too loud in your leisuretime,
And exhaust your lungs in your German bodies,
Otherwise we'll make the variations to your song
With bombs and cannonballs.

Germany

Make as much noise as you like,
You on the left of the Rhine.
But don't throw lead at us,
Otherwise we'll break your arms and legs
And spines and skulls immediately.

The Rhine Crisis, 1840. Cartoon illustrating the reaction in Germany

Questions

1   How and why do documents **1.3** and **1.4** use history to support their arguments?

2   Fichte was rewarded for his utterances; the Burschenschaften were proscribed in **1819**. What similarities and differences are there between Fichte's and von Hase's attitudes towards liberalism and nationalism that could explain this?

3   (i) What was the cartoonist saying about French intention and the German reaction?
    (ii) What can you infer about the cartoonist's attitude towards German nationalism? Explain.

4   Why must historians be careful when talking about liberalism and nationalism in this period?

5   Why did the two ideologies become closely linked? How important a role did they play in the development of Germany in the period 1815–48?

Economic developments

Most historians agree that the economic development of Germany played an essential role in the eventual unification of the country. This development can be traced to the early part of the century, and was due in large part to the work of the Zollverein.

1.6

German cartoon on customs prior to the Zollverein, 1834

1.7 Treaty establishing the Zollverein, March 1833

1 The customs associations at present existing between the before-mentioned States shall, for the future, form one confederation, united by a common system of trade and customs and comprehending all the countries included therein.

4 Similar laws, relative to import, export and transit duties, shall   5
prevail within the dominions of the Contracting States ...

6 Freedom of trade and commerce between the Contracting States, and a common interest in the customs revenues, as settled in the following articles, shall commence with the operation of the present treaty.   10

7 And from the same period, also, all import, export and transit duties shall be discontinued on the common boundaries of the late Prussian and Hessian, and Bavarian and Württemberg associations, and all articles which are already allowed to be freely interchanged in the territory of one, shall be freely, and without restrictions, admitted   15 into the territory of the other, with the following reserved exceptions ...

[The articles that follow deal with these exceptions, the equalisation of internal (i.e. excise) duties, uniformity of road and river tolls, steps to be taken towards uniformity in the monetary system and   20 weights and measures etc.]

22 The amount of duties which are to become common property shall be divided among the Contracting States, according to the population of each State comprehended in the union ...

The census of the population in each separate State of the union   25
shall be taken every three years ...

33 A congress, at which each of the Governments of the union shall appoint a plenipotentiary, shall be held annually ... for the purpose of general discussion ...

41 The present treaty, which is to be brought into operation on 1   30
January 1834, shall continue in force until 1 January 1842.

Annual Register, 1838, in L. Snyder, *Documents of German History*, New York, 1958

1.8   The Zollverein, 1834

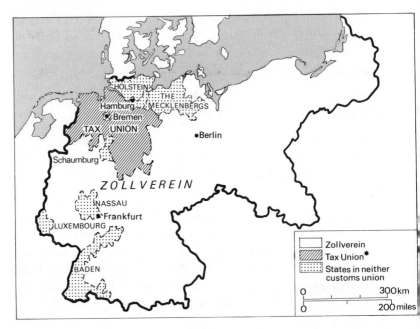

*The Tax Union was what was left of another commercial union called the Middle Union, formed in 1828. It comprised Hanover, Brunswick and Oldenburg, who all refused to join the Zollverein

1.9   The need for railways. Friedrich List, a leading German economist of the time, promotes the building of a railway from Leipzig to Dresden

I could not watch the astonishing effects of railways in England and North America without wishing that my German Fatherland would partake of the same benefits ...

... having settled in Saxony for some years, I determined to devote my leisure time to exploring the relevant local conditions, as far as this is possible for a stranger ... Railways would carry wood, turf and coal at less than half the present costs ... Bavaria, where flour, meat and other foodstuffs are 50–100 per cent cheaper than in Leipzig, could export its surplus to the Erzebirge, the Elbe and the Hansa cities ... Cheaper food and fuel would partly enhance the well-being of the working classes, and partly lower money wages, increase population and increase the extent of industry. Cheap building materials

and low money wages would encourage building and lower the rents
in the new and more distant parts of the city. On the other hand,
increased population and industry would increase the rents, and   15
thereby the value of the houses, in the centre of the city, well placed
for trade and industry. In one word: population, the number of
buildings, industry, trade, and the value of land and houses in
Leipzig would be doubled and in a short space of time, and I do not
doubt for one minute that this increase in value in Leipzig alone   20
would in a few years exceed the total capital costs of the new
railways ...

Memorandum to the Saxon Government from Friedrich List, in Erwin
Beckerath and Otto Stuhler, *Friedrich List, Werke, vol. III, Schriften
zum Verkehrswesen*, Berlin, 1929, pp. 157–65

1.10   Extracts from Friedrich List's, *The National System of Political Economy*, 1841

I was not satisfied with teaching young men the science of political
economy in its present form: I desired also to teach them by what
economic policy the welfare, the culture, and the power of Germany
might be promoted ...

I was led to consider the nature of *nationality*. I perceived that the   5
popular theory took no account of *nations*, but simply of the entire
human race on the one hand, or the single individual on the other. I
saw clearly that free competition between two nations which are
highly civilised can be mutually beneficial only where both of them
are in a nearly equal position of industrial development, and that any   10
nation which ... is getting behind others in industry, commerce and
navigation, must first of all strengthen its own individual powers. In a
word, I perceived the distinction between *cosmopolitical* and *political*
economy. I felt that Germany must abolish her internal tariffs, and
by the adoption of a common uniform policy toward foreigners, strive   15
to attain to the same degree of commercial and industrial development to which other nations have attained by means of their commercial policy ...

I would indicate, as the distinguishing characteristic of my system,
nationality, as the intermediate interest between those of *individualism*   20
and of entire *humanity* ... My sole encouragement lies in the
thought that much will be found in my book that is new and true,

and also somewhat that may serve especially to benefit my German Fatherland ...

Between each individual and entire humanity stands *the nation*, with its special language and literature, with its peculiar origin and history, with its special manners and customs, laws and institutions, with the claims of all of these for existence, independence, perfection, and continuance for the future, and with separate territory. The nation is a society which, united by a thousand ties of mind and of interests, combines itself into one independent whole, which recognises the law of right for within itself, and in its united character is still opposed to other societies of a similar kind in their national liberty, and consequently, under the existing conditions of the world, can only maintain self-existence and independence by its own power and resources ...

The German nation cannot be complete as long as it does not extend over the whole coast, from the mouth of the Rhine to the frontier of Poland, including *Holland* and *Denmark*. A natural consequence of this union must be the admission of both these countries into the German Bund, and consequently into the German nationality, whereby the latter will at once obtain what it is now in need of, namely, fisheries, and naval power, maritime commerce, and colonies. Besides, both these nations belong, as respects their descent and whole character, to the German nationality ...

Friedrich List, *Das nationale System der politischen Okonomie*, Stutt-gart, 1925 pp. xxxix–82 passim

1.11   Tables showing industrial growth in the German Confederation 1815–48 (Austrian and UK figures are given for comparison)

Coal and lignite production: annual average (in million tonnes)

	German Confederation	Austria	UK
1815	1.2	–	16.2
1825–29	1.6	0.2	22.3
1835–39	3.0	0.3	28.1
1845–49	6.1	0.8	48.6

Pig iron production: annual average (in thousand tonnes)

	German Confederation	Austria	UK
1825–29	90	73	669
1835–40	146	103	1,142
1845–49	184	146	1,786

Length of railway line open at the end of each year (in kilometres)

	German Confederation	Austria	UK
1835	6	–	544
1840	469	144	2,390
1845	2,143	728	3,931

Woollen and worsted industry indicators: annual average raw wool output (in thousand tonnes)

	German Confederation	Austria	UK
1814–24	12.7	–	50
1825–34	18.1	–	53
1835–44	25.3	31	56
1845–54	28.2	27	60

Tables based on statistics from C. M. Cipolla, *The Emergence of Industrial Societies*, The Fontana Economic History of Europe, Vol. 4, 1973

Questions

1 Study cartoon **1.6**. What do you think the cartoonist is saying about:
   (i) German customs?
   (ii) German politics?
   Explain your answer.

2 What parts of the Treaty establishing the Zollverein [**1.7**] are specifically designed to overcome the problems indicated in **1.6**? How were these problems to be tackled?

3 What other economic problems did the Zollverein seek to overcome [**1.7**]?

4 (i) Which parts of this treaty [**1.7**] had important political consequences? Explain.

    (ii) What were more important to the architects of the Zollverein: economic or political considerations? Give reasons for your answer.

5   Study the extracts from the works of Friedrich List [**1.9** and **1.10**].

    (i) According to List, what benefits would the development of railways bring?

    (ii) What economic policy does List advocate for Germany in **1.10**? How does he support his arguments?

6   Look at the economic statistics [**1.11**]. How successful was the Zollverein in improving the German Confederation's economic performance by 1845? Did this performance fall short of List's vision in any way? Explain fully.

7   'The mighty lever of German unification.' Do documents **1.6**–**1.11** support this view of the Zollverein?

Metternich

Metternich was the chief architect of the German Confederation. His sole intention was to maintain Austria's domination. He sought to achieve this by repressing threatening ideologies such as nationalism and liberalism, and co-operating with Prussia and the German princes.

1.12   Extracts from the Carlsbad Decrees, 1819

Article 1 There shall be appointed for each university a special representative of the ruler of each state ...

    This representative shall enforce strictly the existing laws and disciplinary regulations; he shall observe with care the attitude shown by the university instructors in their public lectures and registered courses; and he shall, without directly interfering in scientific matters or in teaching methods, give a beneficial direction to the teaching, keeping in view the future attitude of the students. Finally, he shall give increasing attention to everything that may promote morality ... among the students ...

Article 2 The confederated governments mutually pledge themselves to eliminate from the universities or any other public educational institutions all instructors who shall have obviously proved their unfitness for the important work entrusted to them by openly deviating from their duties, or by going beyond the boundaries of their functions, or by abusing their legitimate influence over young minds, or by presenting harmful ideas hostile to public order or subverting existing governmental instructions ...

Article 3 The laws that for some time have been directed against secret and unauthorised societies in the universities shall be strictly   20
enforced. Such laws are applicable especially to the association formed some years ago under the name of Allgemeine Burschen-schaft, for the organisation of that society implies the completely impermissible idea of permanent fellowship and constant intercom-munication between universities. The special representatives of the   25
government are enjoined to exert great care in watching these organi-sations ...

The governments mutually agree that all individuals who shall be shown to have maintained their membership in secret or unauthorised associations, or shall have taken membership in such associations,   30
shall not be eligible for any public office ...

As long as this edict remains in force, no publication which appears daily, or as a serial not exceeding twenty sheets of printed matter, shall be printed in any state of the Confederation without prior knowledge and approval of the state officials ...   35

Printed in L. Snyder, *Documents of German History*, New York, 1958, pp. 158–60

1.13   Extracts from letters from Metternich, outlining his views on (i) revolution, (ii) German revolutionaries and (iii) the German princes

(i) Revolution in its precise sense ... can only have two objects: the transmutation of every kind of private property or a change in the form of government ... What the revolution destroyed in France still exists to a large extent in Germany, and consequently that which has been, so to speak, reduced to ashes in that country still exists as   5
combustible material in Germany.

Letter from Metternich to Thurn, 6 June 1819

(ii) the principle of the fusion of all parts of Germany into one body politic is the real aim, and all at once, there is no denying it, it is the natural desire of the revolutionaries and of a whole crowd of pro-gressive thinkers in Germany. Now, this principle cannot become operative until the political institutions which still separate the different parts of that vast country disappear.

Letter from Metternich to Lebzeltern, the Austrian Ambassador in St Petersburg, 30 Sept 1819

(iii) The more aware states and their princes become of the inferiority of their position in relation to powerful monarchies like Austria and Prussia, the more need they imagine there to be to fortify themselves by alliances and leagues ... We must accept that there is only one alternative; either the states and the peoples of Germany will grow used to finding hopes of peace and security in the natural ties with Austria and Prussia, or they will seek them in foreign connections.

Letter from Metternich to Zichy, the Austrian Ambassador in Berlin, 17 July 1816

Printed in G. de Bertier de Sauvigny, *Metternich and his Times*, London, 1962, pp. 169–71 passim

1.14   Metternich writing on the Zollverein, 1833

The German Confederation cannot be considered a really effective political institution, nor is it possible for it to maintain the high place which it has had on the European political scene, unless it remains completely faithful to the principle of equality of rights and duties among the members of the federal body. Special privileges for any powers whatsoever are banned by the Confederation, as created by the Act of the Congress of Vienna (with exception that the presidence of the Diet is officially recognised as belonging to Austria); all members should exercise with equal liberty and independence their right of voting in the Diet, a right which the constitution guaranteed them ...

The situation has changed as a result of the formation of the Prussian Customs Union. Now a number of independent states accept, in relation to a neighbour superior in power, the obligation of conforming to *its* laws, of submitting to *its* administrative measures and *its* control in a most important branch of public finance. The equality of rights of the members, as arranged in the federal act and maintained until this time, now vanishes ...

Within the great Confederation, a smaller confederation is being
formed, in every meaning of the term, a *status in statu* ... Little by   20
little, under the direction of Prussia and by the necessary formation
of common interests, the states which make up this union will com-
pose a more or less compact body, which in every matter which
comes before the Diet (and not simply in commercial affairs) will act
and vote in common on the basis of prearranged principles. Under   25
such circumstances, there can be no more useful discussion in the
Diet. Such debates will be replaced by votes agreed upon in advance
and motivated, not by the interests of the Confederation, but by the
exclusive rights of Prussia ...

Prussia can be counted upon to utilise all the resources of her   30
political activity. She will use the satisfaction of material interests to
weaken the influence of Austria over the courts dedicated to her
system, to sabotage their relations with Austria, to make them used to
the idea of turning their eyes to Berlin ...

Metternich, *Mémoires*, vol. V, Paris, 1882, pp. 524–28

Questions

1   Explain what the authors of the Carlsbad Decrees [1.12] meant by:
     (i) 'future attitude' [line 8]   (ii) morality [line 9]
     (iii) Article 2
2   What measures did Metternich take to repress ideas he found
     unacceptable? How effective were they?
3   Look at the letters from Metternich [1.13].
     (i) Explain Metternich's view of revolution and how it applies to
         Germany.
     (ii) Why does Metternich think that ties between German princes on
          the one hand and the Prussians and Austrians on the other are so
          important?
4   In what ways does Metternich's attitude towards Prussia differ in
     1.14 from that in 1.13? How do you account for this difference?
5   Why is Metternich so anxious to stress the 'equality of the rights of
     the members' [1.14, line 17]?
6   In the light of the evidence in this chapter, assess how far each of the
     following factors either kept Germany divided or promoted greater
     unity in the period 1815–48:
     (i) The economy   (ii) Metternich   (iii) The German princes
     (iv) German society   (v) The Great Powers

2 1848: 'The Crazy Year'

Complex social, economic and ideological factors combined to produce revolution throughout Europe in 1848. This chapter looks at the underlying causes of the revolution in Germany and its ultimate failure, and asks whether it ever had any chance of success or whether it was doomed from the start. Either way, it certainly had profound implications for Germany after 1850.

The causes of the revolution

2.1 Conditions in Silesia in 1844. The Weaver's rising in Silesia, by teacher Wilhelm Wolff

> Here in the great villages Langenbielau (13,000 inhabitants), and Peterswaldau (5,000 inhabitants), and in the other villages such as Armsdorf, Peilau, etc, cotton weaving particularly is done at home. The distress of the workers was and is not less important here ...
>
> The distress and the urge to obtain work was used by the individual manufacturers to the greatest possible extent in order to obtain a great quantity of goods for little pay. Among these the brothers Zwanziger in Peterswaldau were pre-eminent. For a web of cotton of 140 *ells*, on which a weaver had to work for 9 days and for which other employers paid 32 silver *groschen*, they paid only 15. For 160 ells of fustian, which required 8 full days of strenuous work, they paid a wage of $12\frac{1}{2}$ and 12 silver groschen. Indeed, they declared themselves ready to give work to another 300 weavers prepared to work as much for 10 silver groschen. Bitter misery forced the poor to work even under these conditions. From his 12 or 10 silver groschen respectively, the weaver had to give up $2\frac{1}{2}$ to 3 silver groschen to the bobbin-winder, bear all state, communal and seignorial dues – and live ...
>
> A crowd of weavers appeared in Nieder-Peterswaldau and on its march attracted all weavers from their dwellings on the left and right. Then they went to the not far distant Kapellenberg and formed up

into pairs and moved towards the new residence of the Zwanzigers. They demanded higher pay and – a present! With ridicule and threats this was refused to them. It was not long before the crowd stormed into the house, broke into all chambers, vaults, lofts and cellars and smashed everything, from the splendid mirror windows, trumeaus, chandeliers, tiled stoves, porcelain, furniture, to the staircases; tore up books, bills of exchange and papers, penetrated into the second residence, into the coach houses, into the drying house, to the mangling machine, into the baggage warehouse and threw the goods and stock out of the windows where they were torn up, cut into little pieces and trodden under foot, or – in imitation of the Leipzig mess business – distributed to those standing around. In fear of death Zwanziger fled with his family to Reichenbach ... It was solely the strength of the military power, and the infantry and artillery, and later even the cavalry, that prevented the weavers from trying any further resistance.

Wilhelm Wolff, *Das Elend und der Aufruhr in Schlesien*, 1844, quoted in S. Pollard and C. Holmes, *Documents of European Economic History*, vol. 1, 1958

2.2 Prince Felix Lichnowsky, an aristocrat in Silesia, describes the condition of Silesian weavers, at the Prussian United Diet, 1847

The unfortunate weavers ... when they were no longer able to support themselves by their usual occupation, were forced to work with cotton. Not only in Silesia but also in Westphalia, as I learned only yesterday from Westphalian manufacturers, thousands of workers turned from linen to cotton. There arose consequently such an overproduction that neither employers nor employees could survive. Numerous factories were forced to shut down, others went into bankruptcy. Among these were very many well-intentioned, kind owners who were reluctant to exploit their workers, although their own deficits mounted. Competition declined, and the freedom of the worker disappeared, for the more abundant and varied the articles being produced, the more independent the position of the worker.

Heartless manufacturers oppressed the poor workers, who no longer had the choice of seeking employment with a more humane owner.

This is perhaps the cause of those sad events which have recently taken place in Silesia. I believe it to be hunger, not communistic ideas. He who wants joy in life must have more than his daily bread. He must be able to contemplate tomorrow with a sense of security for himself and his family. As long as there was a sure, and honest livelihood, none of the Silesian weavers paid any attention to communistic agitation. They did not despair of themselves nor of their fate, they did not despair of their King nor of their God. And then at last despair was aroused among them by hunger.

Printed in T. S. Hamerow, *Restoration, Revolution, Reaction,* **Princeton University, 1958, pp. 86–87**

2.3 ᵢ Economic causes of the revolution

(i) Price indices for the German Confederation (1846 = 100)

1840	91	1847	111
1845	93	1848	87
1846	100		

From C. M. Cipolla, *The Emergence of Industrial Societies,* The Fontana Economic History of Europe, Vol. 4, 1973

(ii) Growth of German population 1815–70

1816	24,833,000	1855	36,138,000
1825	28,113,000	1865	39,548,000
1835	30,802,000	1873	42,518,000
1845	34,290,000		

From P. Benaerts, *Les Origines de la Grande Industrie Allemande,* Paris, 1933, p. 136; G. Stolper, *German Economy 1870–1940,* London, 1940, p. 38

(iii) Growth of German cities, 1800–80

	1800	1850	1880
Munich	30,000	110,000	230,000
Cologne	50,000	97,000	145,000
Essen	4,000	9,000	57,000
Chemnitz	14,000	32,000	95,000
Dusseldorf	10,000	27,000	95,000

From W. G. East, *An Historical Geography of Europe,* London, 1935, p. 415

2.4   The Declaration of Heidelberg, 5 March 1848. News of the 1848 revolution in Paris brought about a meeting at Heidelberg of over 50 liberal delegates from 6 German states. This is their declaration:

1.   Heidelberg, 5 March. Today 51 men were assembled here, from Prussia, Bavaria, Würtemberg, Baden, Nassau and Frankfurt, almost all members of state assembles, in order to discuss the most urgent measures for the Fatherland in this moment of decision.

Unanimously resolved in their devotion for the freedom, unity,   5
independence and honour of the German nation, they all express their conviction that the establishment and defence of these highest blessings must be attempted by co-operation of all the German peoples with their governments, so long as delivery is still possible in this manner.   10

The assembled unanimously expressed their conviction of what the Fatherland urgently needs as follows:

Germany must not be involved in war through intervention in the affairs of the neighbouring country or through non-recognition of the changes in the state made there.   15

Germans must not be caused to diminish or rob from other nations the freedom and independence which they themselves ask as their right.

The meeting of a national representation elected in all the German lands according to the number of the peoples must not be postponed,   20
both for the removal of imminent internal and external dangers, and for the development of the strength and flowering of German national life! At the same time they have agreed to concentrate their efforts so that as soon as possible a more complete assembly of men of trust from all German peoples should come together in order to continue   25
deliberation of this most important matter and to offer its co-operation to the Fatherland as well as to the Governments.

A main task of the national representation will in any case be common defence ... and external representation, whereby great sums of money will be saved for other important needs, while at the same   30
time the identity and suitable self-administration of the different states remains in existence.

With the prudent, faithful and manly co-operation of all Germans, the Fatherland may hope to achieve and to maintain freedom, unity and order in the most difficult situations, and joyfully to greet the   35
advent of a hardly expected strength and flowering ...

Printed in A. Stiles. *The Unification of Germany 1815–90*, 1986, pp. 27–28

Questions

1   What are the causes of the workers' misery, according to Wolff [2.1]?
2   How does Lichnowsky's account of the plight of the Silesian weavers [2.2] differ from Wolff's [2.1]? How can you explain this difference?
3   Can the statistics in 2.3 be used to explain the outbreak of revolution in Germany in 1848? In what way?
4   The Declaration of Heidelberg was drawn up by middle-class liberals rather than by workers. How does this show itself in 2.4?
5   What were the main themes of the Heidelberg Declaration?
6   How adequately do sources 2.1–2.4 explain the outbreak of revolution in Germany in 1848? Explain.

The course of the revolution

Violent incidents spread rapidly, forcing governments, including Frederick William IV's in Prussia, to grant liberal constitutions.

2.5

Fighting at the Berlin barricades, 18 March 1848. Engraving from a drawing by J. Kirchhoff, 1848

2.6   Patriotic song, popular in Berlin, March 1848

Black, Red and Gold, these are the colours
We Germans proudly bear on high;
Black, Red and Gold, these are the colours
For which in fight we gladly die.

The Black betokens death to tyrants
Who laughing nailed is to the tree;
And Red's the blood we poured as offering
For justice and for Liberty.

But Gold is freedom's blessing
That men, their duty done, may see,
So fly on highways and on by-ways
The sacred German colours three.

Black, Red and Gold, these are the colours
Fill every German eye with pride;
Black, Red and Gold, with that fair harvest
Teems all the German countryside.

Printed in J. G. Legge, *Rhyme and Revolution in Germany*, London, 1918, p. 242

2.7   Frederick William IV's Proclamation to the German people, 21 March 1848

To my people and to the German nation

With confidence I speak today, when the Fatherland is in the greatest danger, to the German nation, among whose noblest tribes my people may proudly count itself. Germany is in a state of internal ferment and can be threatened by external danger from more than one side. It can be saved from this double, urgent danger only by the most intimate unity of the German princes and peoples under one leadership.

Today I take over this leadership for the days of danger. My people, which does not shirk danger, will not desert me, and

Germany will follow me with confidence. I have today taken the old German colours and have put Myself and My people under the venerable banner of the German Reich. Prussia henceforth merges in Germany. The diet already called for 2 April offers itself as a means and as a lawful organ with which to proceed in conjunction with my people to the rescue and calming of Germany. I intend to invite the princes and estates of Germany, in a force to be considered at once, to meet with organs of this diet in a common assembly. The thus-formed temporary assembly of the German estates will, in common free deliberation, take without delay the necessary precautions regarding the common internal and external danger.

What is needed above all today:

1 The formation of a common German national federal army.

2 The declaration of armed neutrality.

This arming and declaration of the Fatherland will inspire Europe with respect for the sanctity and inviolability of the area of the German tongue and the German name. Only unity and strength will today be able to preserve peace in our beautiful common Fatherland, with its flourishing trade and crafts.

Together with the measures for averting the momentary danger, the assembly of the German estates will deliberate about the rebirth and foundation of a new Germany, of a united, not uniform, Germany, of a unity in diversity, of a unity with freedom.

The general introduction of a truly constitutional constitution with ministerial responsibility, in all the states, public and oral administration of justice in criminal causes based on courts with juries, equal political and civic rights for all religions, confessions, and a truly popular liberal administration, will alone be able to create and to strengthen such a higher and inner unity.

Frederick William
Counts Arnim v. Rohr, Count
Schwerin Bornemann. Arnim. Kühne.

Quoted in L. Snyder, *Documents of German History*, New York, 1958

Questions

1   How does the artist of **2.5** try to evoke sympathy? How effective do you think the illustration is?

2   How does the poet of **2.6** try to appeal to all those involved in revolutionary activity? Explain.

3   Comment on the King's motives in making the following references in **2.7**:
  (i) 'external danger' [**line 5**]
  (ii) 'Prussia henceforth merges in Germany' [**lines 14–15**]
  (iii) 'trade and crafts' [**line 29**]
  (iv) 'Together with the measures for averting the momentary danger, the assembly of the German estates will deliberate about the rebirth and foundation of a new Germany, of a united, not uniform, Germany, of a unity in diversity, of a unity with freedom' [**lines 30–33**]

4   Frederick William IV was widely regarded as a liberal-minded king prior to the revolution. Why did events in 1848 and 1849 cause many to revise this view?

5   Why did Prussia and other German states succumb to the revolutionaries so easily?

2.8   The Kleindeutschland–Grossdeutschland debate

Speech by Heinrich von Gagern, from Bayreuth in Bavaria, President of the Frankfurt Parliament, 26 October 1848

I believe, therefore, ... that we must seek a relationship which would not force Austria to detach its German from its non-German provinces, but would keep it in the most intimate association with   5
Germany. The question is therefore: is it more in the interest of Germany that the whole of Germany should only so organise itself, only engage in so lax a unity, that Austria, without being forced to break up the union of its German and non-German provinces in one state, could belong to the Reich on the same terms as the other   10
German states? Or is it not in the general interests of the nation of Austria as well as of the rest of Germany, that at least the rest of Germany should form a closer connection; even if Austria because of its non-German provinces cannot enter into this narrowest union on the same terms but that nevertheless a close federal relationship be   15
maintained between Austria and the rest of Germany? ... I have,

therefore, in accordance with this view, formulated a motion which I am honoured to announce to the High Assembly:

'In view of its constitutional connection with non-German territories and provinces, Austria remains in permanent and indissoluble union with the rest of Germany. The organic stipulation for this federal relationship made necessary by the changed circumstances will be contained in a special federal act' ...

Quoted in F. Wigard, *Stenographischer Bericht*, vol. IV, pp. 28–96 ff.

2.9   Speech by the radical poet, Uhland, from Tübingen in Württemberg, to the Frankfurt Parliament, 1848

It has been well said that the mission entrusted by Providence to Austria was to dominate the East and to carry to the East enlightenment and civilisation. But how can German Austria exercise this power if it is itself overpowered? How can it light and enlighten if it is itself overshadowed and obscured? Granted that Austria is called to be a lamp to the East, she has another and a higher function, that of 'an artery in Germany's heart'. Austria has been with us in the German Federation, and the pressure of Austrian diplomacy has weighed like a load on Austria herself, on us, and on every movement towards freedom in the individual German states. We would nevertheless not have let Austria go. We knew what we owed to her. But it now appears Austria is to be torn away. Now, when young as an eagle, with the fresh wounds of the March and May battles she approaches us to strike the new treaty of freedom! It is said that ancient walls are indestructible because their lime was mixed with blood; Austria has mingled its heart's blood with the mortar that is to serve for the new structure of German freedom. Austria must be with us and remain with us in the new Paulskirche. Gentlemen, you have only this instant passed a law protecting the personal freedom of the members of this House. Are you going to vote that a hundred and fifty representatives of the Austro-German people shall be driven into exile before your very eyes?

J. G. Legge, *Rhyme and Revolution in Germany*, London, 1918, p. 508

2.10 Vote effectively to exclude Austria from the new Germany, Frankfurt Parliament, 1849

(i)	By region	Yes	No	Abstention	Absent	Total
	Prussia	150	30	0	17	197
	North Germany (excluding Prussia)	72	37	0	14	123
	South Germany	39	69	0	19	127
	Habsburg Empire	0	88	3	20	111
	TOTAL	261	224	3	70	558

(ii)	By political persuasion	Yes	No	Abstention	Absent	Total
	Right	24	5	0	9	38
	Right Centre	163	17	3	22	205
	Left Centre	23	19	0	7	49
	Left	15	117	0	19	151
	Independent	36	66	0	13	115
	TOTAL	261	224	3	70	558

(iii)	By religion	Yes	No	Abstention	Absent	Total
	Protestant	167	69	0	25	261
	Catholic	42	120	3	36	201
	Other	6	7	0	1	14
	Not known	46	28	0	8	82
	TOTAL	261	224	3	70	558

F. Eyck, *The Frankfurt Parliament 1848–49*, 1968, pp. 358–61 passim

Questions

1 How did von Gagern [2.8] and Uhland [2.9] try to win support? Explain by careful reference to the text.
2 Which speech do you think is more convincing, 2.8 or 2.9? Why?
3 Study 2.10. What were the most potent considerations which persuaded the majority of representatives to exclude Austria from a united Germany? Explain fully.
4 What conclusions can historians reach from the tables in 2.10?
5 Why was the decision to exclude Austria from a united Germany so important?
6 Does your wider reading indicate that this decision was the major reason for the Diet's collapse in credibility?

The failure of the revolution

2.11   Rejection of the Imperial Crown by Frederick William IV, 1849

Gentlemen, the message you bring me has deeply moved me. It has directed my gaze to the King of Kings, and to the sacred and august duties I have, as the King of my people, and a Prince among the mightiest in Germany. A look in that direction, gentlemen, gives clearness to the vision and certainty to the heart. In the resolution of the German National Assembly you .have communicated to me, I recognize the voice of the representatives of the German people. Your call gives me a right, the value of which I know how to prize. If accepted, it demands from me incalculable sacrifices, and burdens me with heavy duties. The German National Assembly has counted on me in all things which were calculated to establish the unity of Germany and the power of Prussia. I honour its confidence; please express my thanks for it. I am ready by deeds to prove that their reliance on my loyalty, love and devotion to the cause of the German Fatherland has not been misplaced. But I should not justify that confidence – I should not answer to the expectations of the German people – I should not strengthen the unity of Germany – if I, violating sacred rights and breaking my former explicit and solemn promises, were, without the voluntary assent of the crowned Princes and free States of our Fatherland, to take a resolution which must be of decisive importance to them and to the States which they rule. It will now lie with the several Governments of the German States to examine together the constitution which the National Assembly has drawn up, and declare whether it will be of advantage to each and to all – whether the rights it confers on me will place me in the position to guide with a strong hand, as my position requires, the destinies of Germany and the great German Fatherland, and realize the expectations of the people. But of this, Germany may be certain, and you may declare it in every state – that if it needs the protection of the Prussian sword or shield from external or internal enemies, I will not fail, even without a summons. I shall follow that course from which my royal House and my people have never departed – the course of German loyalty.

Annual Register, 1849, in L. Snyder, *Documents of German History*, 1958

2.12 Declaration by 66 National Assembly representatives, 21 May 1849

With the decision of 28 March of this year the constitution-making of the National Assembly was completed. The signatories below are convinced that this constitution [a constitution for a United German *Reich*] was the only formula, attainable in the given circumstances, for a peaceful solution and a reconciliation of the interests and rights   5 of the various German races, states, and dynasties ... Guided by this conviction, the signatories have so far co-operated in all the decisions, which by the appropriate constitutional means and through public opinion could have brought each individual state to recognise the constitution of the *Reich* ...   10

To their deep grief events have assumed a different complexion and the hopes of the German nation, so near fulfilment, seem likely to miscarry. On one hand, though faced by the very great dangers threatening the Fatherland, four German kings, including the Prussian King himself, have declined the formula of mediation between   15 the conflicting principles threatening our times which the *Reich* constitution offered. On the other hand, a movement of violence has arisen, actually nothing to do with the *Reich* constitution, yet threatening one of its most important sections: that concerned with its supreme head. This movement has arisen in those very states which   20 have already recognised the constitution. Both sides appeal to the arbitrament of force, while the provisional Central Power declares that effective action for the execution of the *Reich* constitution lies outside its functions and duties. Finally, since 10 May, a series of decisions has been taken by a new majority in the Assembly, which   25 are, in part, impossible to execute and, in part, quite contradictory to the course pursued by the earlier majority to which the signatories belonged. In the position of affairs, the National Assembly has only one choice; *either*, by setting aside what has so far been the Central Power, to tear assunder the last common, legal bond between all   30 German governments and peoples, and to foment a civil war, whose beginning has already shaken the foundations of all social order, *or* to renounce the execution of the *Reich* constitution by means of an act of legislation and to do so in co-operation with the provisional Central Power. The signatories have considered the second of these   35 two evils the lesser for the Fatherland...

From P. Wentzcke, *Die erste deutsche Nationalversammlung und ihr Werk*, Munich, 1922, p. 378

2.13   Marx writing on the failure of the 1848 revolution

Thus vanished the German Parliament, and with it the first and last
creation of the Revolution. Its convocation had been the first evidence that there actually *had been* a revolution in January; and it
existed as long as this, the first modern German Revolution, was not
yet brought to a close. Chosen under the influence of the capitalist
class by a dismembered, scattered, rural population, for the most part
only awaking from the dumbness of feudalism, this Parliament served
to bring in one body upon the political arena all the great popular
names of 1820–48, and then to utterly ruin them. All the celebrities
of middle-class liberalism were here collected. The bourgeoisie
expected wonders; it earned shame for itself and its representatives.
The industrial and commercial capitalist class were more severely
defeated in Germany than in any other country; they were first
worsted, broken, expelled from office in every individual state of
Germany, and then put to rout, disgraced and hooted in the Central
German Parliament. Political liberalism, the rule of the bourgeoisie,
be it under a monarchical or republican form of government, is
forever impossible in Germany.

In the latter period of its existence, the German Parliament served
to disgrace forever that section which had ever since March 1848
headed the official opposition, the Democrats representing the
interests of the small-trading, and partially of the farming class. That
class was, in May and June 1849, given a chance to show its means of
forming a stable Government in Germany. We have seen how it
failed; not so much by adverse circumstances as by the actual and
continued cowardice in all trying movements that had occurred since
the outbreak of the revolution; by showing in politics the same short-
sighted, pusillanimous, wavering spirit, which is characteristic of its
commercial operations. In May 1849 it had, by this course, lost the
confidence of the real fighting mass of all European insurrections, the
working class. But yet, it had a fair chance. The German Parliament
belonged to it, exclusively, after the Reactionists and Liberals had
withdrawn. The rural population was in its favour. Two-thirds of the
armies of the smaller states, one-third of the Prussian army, the
majority of the Prussian *Landwehr* [reserve or militia], were ready to
join it, if it only acted resolutely, and with that courage which is the
result of a clear insight into the state of things. But the politicians
who led on this class were not more clear-sighted than the host of

petty tradesmen which followed them. They proved even to be more infatuated, more ardently attached to delusions voluntarily kept up,   40 more credulous, more incapable of resolutely dealing with facts than the Liberals. Their political importance, too, is reduced below the freezing-point. But not having actually carried their common-place principles into execution, they were, under *very* favourable circumstances, capable of a momentary resurrection, when this last hope was   45 taken from them, just as it was from their colleagues of the 'pure democracy' in France by the *coup d'état* of Louis Bonaparte.

K. Marx, *Revolution and Counter Revolution*, 1852

Questions

1   What reasons does Frederick William IV give in **2.11** for rejecting the German crown? Consider whether these were his real reasons. If not, what might his real reasons have been?

2   The Declaration [**2.12**] was issued by the few delegates left in Frankfurt by May 1849. To what did they ascribe the failure of the revolution? How valid do you find their conclusions?

3   Karl Marx wrote about the revolution from the vantage point of 1852 [**2.13**].
How justified was he in arguing that:
   (i) 'The bourgeoisie expected wonders; it earned shame for its representatives' [**lines 10–11**]?
   (ii) 'We have seen how it failed; not so much by adverse circumstances as by the actual and continued cowardice in all trying movements that had occurred since the outbreak of the revolution; by showing in politics the same short-sighted, pusillanimous, wavering spirit...' [**lines 24–28**]?

4   Which source gives a more realistic explanation for the failure of the revolution: **2.11**, **2.12** or **2.13**? Explain your choice.

5   What other factors do you think might have prevented the revolutionaries from uniting Germany?

6   Did the Frankfurt Parliament ever have any chance of achieving its goals? Justify your conclusions.

7   'The revolution of the intellectuals.' Discuss the historian Namier's verdict on 1848 as it applies to Germany.

3 The changing balance 1849–62

With the collapse of the revolution the hopes of the liberals lay in ruins. The 1850s are often called the 'quiet years' by historians. Beneath the surface, however, powerful forces were at work, shifting the focus of German unity from Vienna to Berlin. This chapter deals with the major political and economic developments of the period, culminating with the emergence of Otto von Bismarck.

Political developments, 1849–59

Proposal and counter proposal for change in Germany's political structure followed throughout the 1850s, following the failure of the revolution. Three are considered here. The first was Prussia's attempt to seize the initiative in 1849 and take a lead in German affairs; the second was Austria's response to the burgeoning political power of the Zollverein; the third was the demands of the Nationalverein, the liberal organisation formed in 1859 to promote German unification under Prussian domination.

3.1 Radowitz initiates a plan for Prussia to dominate Germany: a proposed treaty, the Erfurt Union, 26 May 1849

The Governments of Prussia, Saxony and Hanover have concluded the following treaty:

1 The Royal Governments of Prussia, Saxony and Hanover conclude, in compliance with Article 11 of the German Act of Confederation of 8 June 1815, an alliance with the purpose of safeguarding the internal and external security of Germany and the independence and inviolability of the several German States ...

2 All members of the German Confederation may join this alliance ...

3 (1) The supreme direction of the measures which are to be taken to achieve the aims of the alliance is vested in the Crown of Prussia ...

(2) An administrative council, to which all members shall send one or more representatives, shall be formed to conduct the business of the Alliance.

(3) The Administrative Council may take a final decision on the   15
following matters:
  (i) The admission of new members to the Alliance.
  (ii) Steps for the calling of a constituent Reichstag and the direction of its deliberations.
  (iii) The appointment and direction of civil commissioners to be   20
  attached to the military when requests for assistance against
  internal disturbances are made.

4 Should there be diplomatic negotiations ... they shall be conducted
by the Crown of Prussia, and the Administrative Council shall be
kept informed of their progress ...   25

Quoted in L. Snyder, *Documents of German History*, New York, 1958

3.2   Proposals of Bruck, Austrian Minister of Commerce, for a Central European Customs Union

Austria has, above all, one thing *to prevent, namely that, the Zollverein, due to expire at the end of 1852, should be renewed before the
Austro-German Customs Union is irrevocably settled on a sure foundation.* Such a renewal would bind all the German states for twelve
years longer to Prussia's will in all national economic affairs. If   5
Prussia were to see her supremacy assured for so long a time, she
would scarcely be persuaded to enter the Customs Union with Austria – even though it offered the most convincing economic advantages – and to share, to that degree, her supremacy with her. The
matter would, however, stand quite differently, if the renewal of the   10
Zollverein were put in question by several of its members, or if it
were made dependent upon the previous achievement of a Customs
Union with Austria; for rather than endanger the intellectual and
economic supremacy that she gained through the Zollverein, Prussia
would prefer an attempt to share it with Austria ...   15
  The advantages that Germany might expect from such Customs
Union would be: the moral unity which the same tariff and commercial laws, the common administration of these affairs, and an unob-
structed internal economy would stimulate; closer political links; a
large market; complementary industries in the various states, streng-   20
thening and stimulating each other; greater power and still greater
standing abroad; the multiplication of shipping routes and a most

remunerative overseas trade; finally, the satisfaction of the just wishes and expectations of the nation, to whom would be assured all the advantages of German unity without the dangerous disadvantages to particularist interests. Perhaps one might also mention that Austria herself, notwithstanding the political differences still outstanding, unreservedly offers her hand to help forward this unity, because she does not wish to withhold these advantages from the nation any longer and because she hopes to succeed through this unity in settling agitation on other matters ...

Letter from Bruck to Schwarzenberg, 1850, quoted in H. Böhme, *The Foundation of the German Empire*, **1978**

3.3   The Programme of the Nationalverein, August 1859

The present dangerous situation of Europe and of Germany and the need to subordinate the demands of political parties to the great common task of German unification, have brought together from the various German states a number of men, some of them belonging to the democratic party, some to the constitutional party, for the purpose of coming to an understanding about the establishment of a constitution for a united Germany and about the necessary common course of action for the attainment of that aim. They have agreed on the following points:

1 In the present position of the world we see great dangers threatening the independence of our German Fatherland – these are increased rather than diminished by the peace just concluded between France and Austria.

2 These dangers have their ultimate origin in the faulty constitution of Germany and they can be countered only by a speedy alteration of it.

3 For this purpose it is necessary that the German Federal Diet should be replaced by a firm, strong, permanent central government and that a German national assembly should be summoned.

4 In the present circumstances effective steps for the attainment of this aim can originate only with Prussia. We shall, therefore, work to the end that Prussia may take the initiative.

5 Should Germany in the immediate future be again directly threatened from outside, the command of her military forces and her

diplomatic representation abroad shall be transferred to Prussia,   25
pending a definitive constitution of the German central government.

6 It is the duty of every German to support the Prussian government
according to his strength, in so far as its exertions are based upon the
assumption that the tasks of the Prussian state and the tasks and
needs of Germany coincide in essentials and in so far as it directs its   30
activity to the introduction of a strong, free constitution for the whole
of Germany.

7 We expect all patriots in the German Fatherland, whether they
belong to the democratic or to the constitutional party, to place
national independence and unity above party demands and to work   35
together in harmony and perseverance for the attainment of a strong
constitution for Germany.

Quoted in W. Mommsen, *Deutsche Parteiprogramme*, 1960, p. 131

Questions

1   Why does the Erfurt Union plan [3.1] cite Article 11 of the Act of
Confederation [line 4]? Refer to the German Act of Confederation
[1.2] to help you answer this. Was this the real reason for the plan?
What parts of the plan reveal Radowitz's real intentions and why?

2   Compare Metternich's views on the Zollverein in 1833 [1.14] and
Bruck's views in 1850 [3.2]. To what extent did Metternich's fears
prove to be justified? How does Bruck intend to persuade other
German states to agree to his plans for an Austro–German Customs
Union?

3   Both Radowitz's plans [3.1] and Bruck's [3.2] failed. Why do you
think this was?

4   Study the programme of the Nationalverein [3.3]. Comment on the
significance of the following:
  (i) Article 1
  (ii) 'faulty constitution ...' [line 14]
  (iii) Articles 4 and 7

5   What do documents 3.1–3.3 tell us about:
  (i) Changes in Prussian and Austrian relations in the 1850s?
  (ii) Nationalism and liberalism in the same period?
Why did these changes take place? How important did they prove to
be in the 1860s?

Economic developments

The most significant development in the 1850s for the future of Germany, however, was the strengthening of the Prussian and German economy. This was due to the advantages conferred by the Zollverein, and by the location of copious raw materials in the Saar and Ruhr Valleys and in Silesia. Austria, on the other hand, was economically weak. She possessed few raw materials and remained industrially backward in an age where industrial strength was of increasing importance.

Figures for the period from 1850 right up to 1870 are included here in order to avoid fragmenting them in later chapters. They should be re-examined when Chapters 4, 5 and 6 are looked at.

3.4   Tables showing industrial growth in the German Confederation. Austrian and UK figures are given for comparison

Coal and lignite production: annual average (in million tonnes)

	German Confederation	Austria	UK
1850–54	9.2	1.2	50.2
1855–59	14.7	2.2	67.8
1860–64	20.8	3.6	86.3
1865–69	31.0	5.3	104.7

Pig iron production: annual averages (in thousand tonnes)

	German Confederation	Austria	UK
1850–54	245	173	2,716
1855–59	422	226	3,583
1860–64	613	216	4,219
1865–69	1,012	227	4,984

Length of railway line open (in kilometres)

	German Confederation	Austria	UK
1850	5,856	1,579	9,797
1855	7,826	2,145	11,744
1860	11,084	4,543	14,603
1865	13,900	5,858	18,439
1870	18,876	9,589	21,558 (1871)

Woollen and worsted industry: raw wool output (in thousand tonnes)

	German Confederation	Austria	UK
1855–64	31.1	29	65
1865–74	35.2	35	72

From C. M. Cipolla, *The Emergence of Industrial Societies*, The Fontana Economic History of Europe, vol. 4, 1973

Questions

1 Using the figures in 3.4, show how German economic strength grew after 1850.
2 How might each of the following factors have helped German economic growth:
  (i) The Zollverein
  (ii) Prussia's geography
  (iii) new industries
  (iv) the development of banking
  (v) the growth of railways?
3 'Germany was economically united a decade before she became politically united.' Discuss.

Otto von Bismarck

Bismarck was called to office in 1862 to help save the King in the constitutional crisis which threatened the very existence of the Prussian monarchy. An extreme right-wing politician, Bismarck sought to defend Prussian and Junker interests, at all costs. Prior to 1854 he had been in favour of co-operation between Austria and Prussia in the repression of radical political movements, a system that had been founded by Metternich. He now advocated a far more confident and independent role for Prussia. Some historians have subsequently associated Bismarck with the notion of *realpolitik*, a realistic and opportunist approach that characterised his statesmanship. Other historians have tried to portray Bismarck as a master planner of events. This section tackles both these ideas.

3.5   Bismarck writing on Prussian policy towards Germany and Austria, from a memo to his government, 1858

Opinions may differ as to whether or not a close alliance with Austria be desirable. But experience permits no doubt that pliancy and assurances of friendship are not the means by which Prussia can succeed in living upon endurable, not to mention secure, terms with Austria. Gratitude for favours received, patriotic sympathies – in a word, *feelings* of any description, do not guide the policy of Austria. Her interests constrain her to fight against and detract from Prussia's prestige and influence in Germany to the best of her ability. If Prussia takes up a position independent of the Confederation, she will become, by virtue of her intrinsic force, the natural centre of crystallization for those connections of which her neighbours stand in as urgent need as herself. In such connections she will be backed up by the weight of her greatness and speciality as a purely German state, as well as by the similarity of her requirements and developments to those of the German people at large. The neighbouring federal states will endeavour to come to an understanding with her for these reasons, as soon as they shall be firmly convinced that Prussia will not agree to any of the more favourable conditions they had theretofore expected to obtain from her through the agency of the Confederation. They will be all the more conciliatory and easy to manage when they shall have recognised that Prussia is ready to bear, in every respect, with the inconvenience of an isolated position, rather than allow them to dictate laws to her for the regulation of her own behaviour and interests. Those inconveniences, for most of them – particularly for Saxony, Brunswick, both Hesses and Nassau, by reason of their smallness, land-bound situation and frontier conditions – are much harder to endure *à la longue* than for Prussia, whether they concern customs uniformity, railway projects, common exchange and trade laws, postal arrangements, paper currency, banking business or any of the other subjects which the Austrian presidency and the majority states propose to submit to the federal legislature.

But, even if Prussia should not succeed in this enterprise, she has more to hope from the independent exertion of her own strength than from protracted tolerance of her adversaries' federal policy.

Moritz Busch, *Our Chancellor: Sketches for a Historical Picture*, New York, 1884, vol. I, pp. 344–47

3.6 Bismarck in conversation with Disraeli at a dinner given in the Russian Embassy at the time of the International Exhibition in London in 1862, before he came to power. Account from Count Eckstadt, the Saxon Ambassador in London

> 'I shall soon', said in effect the Prussian statesman, 'be compelled to undertake the conduct of the Prussian Government. My first care will be to organise the army, with or without the help of the Landtag. The King was right in undertaking this task, but he cannot accomplish it with his present advisers. As soon as the army have been   5
> brought into such a condition as to inspire respect, I shall seize the first best pretext to declare war against Austria, dissolve the German Diet, subdue the minor states, and give national unity to Germany under Prussian leadership.'

Count Vitzthum von Eckstadt, *St Petersburg and London in the Years 1852–64*, London, 1887, vol, II, p. 172

Questions

1   What policy does Bismarck advocate for Prussia in document 3.5, regarding:
     (i) Austria
     (ii) Other German states?
2   What evidence of *realpolitik* does 3.5 provide?
3   How does the image of Bismarck presented in 3.6 differ from that presented in 3.5? How do you account for this difference?
4   Some historians have cited 3.6 as evidence of Bismarck as a master planner. Many others have dismissed it. What light, if any, does document 3.6 shed on Bismarck's political intentions and motivations?
5   Bismarck changed from being in favour of close co-operation with Austria to being hostile towards her. This happened in 1854. What circumstances do you think may have brought about this change?

The constitutional crisis

The constitutional crisis in Prussia saw Bismarck's *realpolitik* in action. He first infuriated the liberal-dominated Lower House by ignoring them and then outmanoevred them using the 'gap in the constitution' theory.

3.7   Bismarck recounts his appointment by William I

His Majesty concluded by repeating that he could not govern without
suitable ministers.

I replied that His Majesty had been acquainted ever since May
with my readiness to enter the Ministry; I was certain that Roon
would remain with me on his side, and I did not doubt that we
should succeed in completing the cabinet, supposing other members
should feel themselves compelled to resign on account of my
admission. After a good deal of consideration and discussion, the
King asked me whether I was prepared as minister to advocate the
reorganisation of the army, and when I assented he asked me further
whether I would do so in opposition to the majority in parliament
and its resolutions. When I asserted my willingness, he finally
declared, 'Then it is my duty, with your help, to attempt to continue
the battle, and I shall not abdicate' ...

The King invited me to accompany him into the park ...

I succeeded in convincing him that, so far as he was concerned, it
was not a question of Liberal or Conservative of this or that shade,
but rather monarchial rule or parliamentary government, and that the
latter must be avoided at all costs, if even by a period of dictatorship.
I said; 'in this situation I shall, even if your Majesty command me to
do things which I do not consider right, tell you my opinion quite
openly; but if you finally persist in yours, I will rather perish with
the King than forsake your Majesty in the contest with parliamentary
government.' This view was at that time strong and absolute in me,
because I regarded the negations and phrases of the Opposition of
that day as politically disastrous in face of the national task of
Prussia, and because I cherished such strong feelings of devotion and
affection for William I, that the thought of perishing with him
appeared to me, under the circumstances, a natural and congenial
conclusion to my life.

Bismarck, *Reflections and Reminiscences*, written by Bismarck in his
retirement 1891–98, vol. I, pp. 142–34

3.8   Bismarck's 'Blood and Iron Speech' to the Budget Commission of the Prussian Landtag, 25 September 1862

[Bismarck said] he would gladly agree to the budget for 1862, but
without giving any prejudicial explanation. A misuse of constitutional
powers could happen on any side, and would lead to a reaction from
the other side. The Crown, for example, could dissolve [parliament] a
dozen times, and that would certainly be in accordance with the letter 5
of the Constitution, but it would be a misuse. In the same way it can
challenge the budget cancellation as much as it likes: but the limit is
difficult to set: shall it be 6 million, or 60 million? There are
members of the National Union, a party respected because of the
justice of its demands, highly esteemed members, who considered all 10
standing armies superfluous. Now what if a national assembly were of
this opinion! Wouldn't the government have to reject it? People speak
of the 'sobriety' of the Prussian people. Certainly the great independence of the individual makes it difficult in Prussia to rule with the
constitution. In France it is different; the independence of the indivi- 15
dual is lacking there. A constitutional crisis is not shameful, but
honourable. Furthermore we are perhaps too 'educated' to put up
with a constitution; we are too critical; the ability to judge government measures and bills of the National Assembly is too widespread;
there are in the country too many subversive elements who have an 20
interest in revolutionary change. This may sound paradoxical, but it
goes to show how difficult it is in Prussia to carry on a constitutional
existence ... We are too ardent, we like to carry too heavy a weight of
armour for our fragile bodies; but we should also make use of it.
Germany doesn't look to Prussian liberalism, but to its power: 25
Bavaria, Württemberg, Baden can indulge in liberalism, but no one
will expect them to undertake Prussia's role; Prussia must gather and
consolidate her strength in readiness for the favourable moment,
which has already been missed several times; Prussia's boundaries
according to the Vienna treaties are not favourable to a healthy 30
political life; not by means of speeches and majority verdicts will the
great decisions of the time be made – that was the great mistake of
1848 and 1849 – but by iron and blood ...

Quoted in *Bismarck: Die Gesammelten Werke*, ed. H. von Petersdorff et.
al, Berlin, 1923

3.9

'Constitution: I cannot rule with this'

Cartoon from the liberal magazine *Kladderadatsch*

3.10   Bismarck's speech to the House of Representatives concerning the 'gap in the constitution', 27 January 1863

Article 99 reads, if I remember correctly: all income and expenditure of the state must be estimated each year in advance and brought together in a state budget.

If it followed that 'the latter will be fixed annually by the Lower
House' then you were entirely correct in your complaints in the   5
address, for the constitution would be violated. But the text of Article
99 continues: The budget will be fixed annually by law. Now, Article
62 states with incontrovertible clarity how a law is passed. It says that
for the passage of law, including a budget law, agreement of the
Crown and of both Houses is necessary. That the Upper House is   10
justified in rejecting a budget approved by the Lower House but not
acceptable to the Upper is, moreover, emphasised in the article.

Each of these three concurrent rights is in theory unlimited, one as
much as the other. If agreement among the three powers is not
reached, the constitution is lacking in any stipulation about which one   15
must give in. In earlier discussions one passed over this difficulty
with ease; it was assumed according to analogy of other countries,
whose constitution and laws, however, are not published in Prussia
and have no validity here, that the difficulty could be settled with the
two other factors giving in to the Lower House, that if agreement   20
over the budget is not reached between the Crown and the Lower
House, the Crown not only submits to the Lower House and dis-
misses the ministers who do not have the confidence of the Lower
House, but in case of disagreement with the Lower House the Crown
also forces the Upper House by mass appointments to place itself on   25
the plane of the Lower House. In this way, to be sure, the sovereign
and exclusive rule of the Lower House would be established; but
such exclusive rule is not constitutional in Prussia. The constitution
upholds the balance of the three legislative powers on all questions,
also with respect to the budget. None of these powers can force the   30
others to give way. The constitution therefore points to the way of
compromise for an understanding. A statesman of constitutional
experience has said that the entire constitutional life is at every
moment a series of compromise. If the compromise is thwarted in
that one of the participating powers wishes to enforce its own views   35
with doctrinaire absolutism, the series of compromises will be inter-
rupted and in its place will occur conflicts. And since the life of a
state cannot remain still, conflicts become questions of power.
Whoever has the power in hand goes ahead with his views, for the
life of a state cannot remain still even a moment ...   40

Quoted in E. N. Anderson, *The Social and Political Conflict in Prussia
1858–1864*, University of Nebraska, 1954, pp. 218–20

Questions

1   Bismarck wrote **3.7** many years after the event took place. How might this affect its value to us as a piece of historical evidence?

2   In what ways is Bismarck trying to make peaceful overtures to the Landtag in his speech [**3.8**]? What parts of the speech reveal his real intentions? What different interpretations could be placed on the last sentence?

3   How do **3.9** and **3.10** demonstrate Bismarck's attitude towards the constitution? Which do you think is the more accurate, and why?

4   What was the 'gap' in the constitution? How does Bismarck defend his actions? How strong is his argument?

5   What can we learn about German politics in 1862 from documents **3.7–3.10**?

6   Why did Prussian influence in Germany increase and Austria's influence decline in the decade after 1850?

7   'The German Empire was not founded on blood and iron, but on coal and iron' (J. M. Keynes). Discuss.

8   Assess the importance of the following in the history of Germany after 1850:
   (i)   The Crimean War
   (ii) The Austro–Italian War 1859
   (iii) The accession of William I in Prussia in 1860

9   Examine the evolution of Bismarck's political ideas up to 1862.

4 Bismarck, Austria and the North German Confederation

By 1863, Prussia possessed several important strengths compared with Austria. Bismarck sought to elevate Prussia's position in Germany at Austria's expense, and this chapter will show how he succeeded in this, and the widespread impact this had throughout Germany. Again, the question arises: was Bismarck a master-planner, or did he exploit opportunities as they arose? What were his motives at each stage? The three sections in this chapter deal with Austro–Prussian relations and the war with Denmark; the war with Austria; and finally with the political situation after the Prussian victory in 1866.

Austro–Prussian relations and the war with Denmark

The Austrian government was alarmed at Bismarck's appointment. In 1863 Austria sought to reform the German Confederation at a Conference of Princes at Frankfurt in such a way that would reinforce her hegemony. Bismarck managed to persuade the King not to go and relations between the two powers subsequently worsened. However, this did not prevent Bismarck from coaxing Austria into co-operation over the Schleswig-Holstein affair, which presented Bismarck with many political opportunities.

4.1 Bismarck persuades William not to attend the Frankfurt Congress of Princes, 1863

> It was not an easy task to persuade the King to stay away from
> Frankfurt. I exerted myself for that purpose during our drive from
> Wildbad to Baden, when, on account of the servants on the box, we
> discussed the German question in the small open carriage in French.
> By the time we reached Baden I thought I had convinced my master.   5
> But there we found the King of Norway, who was commissioned by
> all the princes to renew the invitation to Frankfurt 29 August. My
> master did not find it easy to resist that move. He reflected over and
> over again: 'Thirty reigning princes and a King to take their
> messages!' Besides, he loved and honoured the King of Saxony, who   10
> moreover of all the princes had personally most vocation for such a

mission. Not until midnight did I succeed in obtaining the King's signature to a refusal to the King of Saxony. When I left my master, both he and I were ill and exhausted by the nervous tension of the situation...

On the return journey from Baden-Baden to Berlin 31 August the King passed so near to Frankfurt that his decision not to take part in the Congress became known to every one. The majority, or at least the most powerful, of the princes felt very uncomfortable at this time when they thought of the scheme of reform which, if Prussia held aloof, left them standing alone with Austria in a connexion where they got no protection from the rivalry of the two Great Powers. The Vienna Cabinet must have thought of the possibility that the other Federal princes would agree in the Congress to the proposals made on 17 August, even when they had been finally left alone with Austria in the reformed federal relation. Otherwise it would not have been demanded of the princes who remained at Frankfurt that they should accept the Austrian proposals and carry them into practice without the consent of Prussia. But at Frankfurt the middle states did not desire either a solely Prussian or a solely Austrian leadership; they wanted to hold as influential a position as arbiters in the sense of the Triad, by which each of the two Great Powers would be driven to compete for the votes of the middle states. To demand of Austria that they should conclude without Prussia they replied by referring to the necessity of fresh negotiations with Prussia and by announcing their own inclination to such a course. The form of their reply to the wishes of Austria was not smooth enough not to excite some irritation at Vienna. The effect on Count Rechberg, prepared by the friendly relations in which our acting as colleagues at Frankfurt had ended, was to make him say that the road to Berlin was not longer or more difficult for Austria than for the middle states.

Bismarck, *Reflections and Reminiscences*, vol. 1, written by Bismarck in his retirement 1891–98, pp. 212–13

4.2   Bismarck co-operates with Austria over Schleswig-Holstein. His views are presented to the Austrians: letter sent to Vienna with General Manteuffel in 1863

We owe it to public opinion in the army and among the people, to carry out our programme resolutely and completely, to assert our power and influence in Germany, and not to yield to any direct

attacks from the Lesser States. The notion of Austria and Prussia
together, that they should share in the Confederate chastisement in   5
Holstein, must be accepted by the Confederation: the Lesser States
must learn that if they attempt to subject the European policy of
Austria and Prussia to the control of the majority of the Confederation they will make the continuance of such Confederate relations
impossible for these two Powers.   10

Quoted in Heinrich von Sybel, *The Founding of the German Empire by
William I*, New York, 1891, vol. 1, p. 458

4.3 Bismarck's motives in the Schleswig-Holstein affair: from a letter to Golz, the Prussian ambassador to France

I utterly repudiate your remark that an 'in itself very simple question
of Prussian policy' is obscured by the dust that the Danish affair is
raising and the phantasmagoria associated with it. The question is
whether we are a great power or a German federal state, and whether
we in accordance with the first conception are to be ruled monarchi-   5
cally or, as is possible in the second case by professors, district and
provincial gossips ... Austria, to our detriment, has always recognised
that with reference to herself, she will not allow herself to be wrested
from her European alliances, if she has any, by the farce which she is
playing out with German sympathies ... If we go too far for her, she   10
will pretend to go along with us a little way, especially will sign what
we do; but the twenty per cent of Germans that she has in her
population are not in the last resort to be an element constraining her
to let herself be carried away by us against her own interest. At the
proper moment she will stay behind us, and will know how to find   15
her proper line towards a European situation as soon as we give it
up ... Never before has the policy of Vienna been controlled to such a
degree *en gros et en détail* from Berlin ... If we now turn our back
upon the Great Powers in order to throw ourselves into the arms of
the policy of the minor states – enmeshed as it is in the net of club- 20
democracy – that would be the most wretched position, either at
home or abroad, to which the monarchy could be brought. We
should be pushed instead of pushing; we should lean for support
upon elements which we do not control, which are necessarily hostile
to us, and to which we should have to devote ourselves uncondition-   25
ally. You believe that there is some hidden virtue in 'German public

opinion', chambers, newspapers, and such like, which might support
or help us in a 'union' of 'hegemony' policy. I consider that a radical
error, a product of the fancy. Our strength cannot proceed from a
press and parliamentary policy, but only from the policy of a great
military power ...

You speak of a conglomeration of states of seventy million people,
with a million soldiers, who are to defy Europe united and compact.
Consequently you attribute to Austria a persistence, dead or alive, in
a policy which must lead to the hegemony of Prussia. Yet you would
not trust further than you could reach her the state which possesses
thirty-five of these seventy millions. Neither would I; but I consider
it our correct policy at present to have Austria with us. Whether the
moment of separation comes and on whose initiative it will come, we
shall see ... I am ... by no means shy of war – quite the reverse; I am
also as indifferent to 'revolutionary' or 'Conservative' as I am to all
phrases. Perhaps you will very soon be convinced that war is also part
of my programme ...

Bismarck, *Reflections and Reminiscences*, 1898 vol. II, pp. 2–4,6

4.4

BRIGANDS DIVIDING THE SPOILS.

'The Prussian bully takes his share of the plunder'

Cartoon from *Punch*, 1864

Questions

1   What was Bismarck's argument with the King [4.1]?
    Why did he find it so difficult to win the argument? Explain.
2   What does 4.1 tell you about Bismarck's attitude towards:
    (i) the Diet
    (ii) Austria?
3   What various justifications does Bismarck give for Austro–Prussian
    co-operation in 4.2 and 4.3? Does 4.1 suggest he may have had
    different motives from those given in 4.2 and 4.3?
4   What can you infer from the passage, '... but I consider it our correct
    policy at present to have Austria with us ... Perhaps you will very
    soon be convinced that war is also part of my programme... [4.3,
    lines 37–43]?
5   Study cartoon 4.4.
    (i) Identify the three characters.
    (ii) What point is the cartoonist making?
    (iii) How fair is this interpretation?
6   How far do these documents [4.1–4.4] support the following
    statements:
    (i) 'Bismarck was unpopular both inside and outside Germany at
    this time.'
    (ii) 'Bismarck was an opportunist who exploited an uncertain situa-
    tion in Denmark and gained a great deal.' Justify your
    conclusions.

War with Austria

Tension between Prussia and Austria continued and intensified after
Gastein; war, it seemed, was inevitable. But Bismarck did not feel strong
enough to risk this in 1865. Conditions changed, however, especially in
relation to France and Italy, and war between Prussia and Austria broke
out in the summer of the following year. It was a very short affair and its
outcome astonished many, not least Napoleon III, who envisaged a
protracted conflict after which he could preside as arbiter of Europe. In
defeating Austria, Bismarck still had an eye on the future.

4.5   Austria recognises difficulties in her relations with Prussia: letters from the Austrian foreign minister, Rechberg, to Bismarck in 1865

(i) Permit me, honoured friend, to express my opinion openly. In all these matters the attitude of the Imperial Cabinet is conditioned by a slight, but I fear increasing, tendency to let small states look upon Austria as a bulwark against Prussia ...

But the more influence the elements thus indicated have upon the course of Austria's policy, the nearer were we brought to the old ruts in which Austria and Prussia were held fast for more than ten years, to the injury of both. We shall succeed in the task you propose for us, only if we keep our connection animated with the fresh life of an *active* common policy such as we have pursued hitherto during this year.

Letter from Rechberg to Bismarck, 6 September 1865

(ii) You know that I give myself with my whole soul to the task of maintaining in the future the harmony that has once more been brought about between Austria and Prussia ... You will grant to me, most honoured friend, that a sincere and loyal recognition of Austria's oneness with Germany is one of those essential conditions without which Austria cannot feel at home in the Prussian alliance. This fact gives the answer to the question, what inexplicable magic is contained for us in the simple word 'tariff-union'. The value of this word is, I admit, one of those things that are imponderable, but the value of our position as a *German Power* is also imponderable [*marginal note by Bismarck:* More *Power* than *German*] ...

The present question, whether Austria shall withdraw from her right to be included in a tariff-union, and thus acknowledge that in a politico-commercial connection she does not belong to Germany [*marginal note by Bismarck:* To the Tariff-union], I must, as an Austrian Minister, answer in the negative ... If we persist in our claim to a tariff-union, it is ... because Austria is a German Power, and cannot allow a common German institution to be closed to her on principle, nor permit herself to be treated as a foreign nation by her own associates in the Confederation.

Letter from Rechberg to Bismarck, 17 September 1865, Heinrich von Sybel, *The Founding of the German Empire by William I*, New York, 1891, vol. III, pp. 457–9

4.6 Bismarck meets Napoleon III at Biarritz. Letter from Bismarck to William I, 1863

They had exaggerated in Paris the importance of the Gastein agreement for the general policy of Prussia, especially as they could not believe that a result which was so advantageous to Prussia had not been purchased by some secret concessions to Austria. The Emperor let it be seen that the Austrian communication, which had reached   5 him by very confidential channels, (apparently through Her Majesty the Empress) had supported the hypothesis of a secret understanding of the German Powers, directed as a sort of coalition against France. Again His Majesty solemnly put the question to me, whether we had not given Austria some guarantee about Venetia. I denied it ...   10 moreover, I thought it impossible that we would conclude an agreement in the future whereby Austria could make a war in which Prussia would have to join without advantage to herself. The Emperor thereupon assured me that he did not intend to initiate any plans which might disturb the peace of Europe ... Using almost the   15 very words in which I had voiced the [same] sentiment to Minister Drouyn de Lhuys, and which the latter had doubtless passed on meanwhile, he said, one must not seek to fashion events, but let them mature themselves; they would not fail to happen, and would then prove that Prussia and France were the two states in Europe whose   20 interests were bound up with one another to the greatest degree, and that he would always be ready to give practical proof of the sympathy and friendship he felt for Prussia. The Emperor then asked what arrangement we proposed to come to with Austria over Holstein. I answered frankly that we hoped to secure and keep Holstein by   25 paying an indemnity. His Majesty made no objection to this, and expressly declared his agreement with the reasons I gave for refuting the anxiety of Minister Drouyn de Lhuys concerning the growth of Prussian power without any equivalent for France. I emphasized the point that the acquisition of the Elbe Duchies was not itself a   30 strengthening of Prussian power; on the contrary, by deploying our navy and developing our defensive position northwards it would tie up the forces of our Fatherland in more than one direction to an extent which would not be compensated by the addition of a million inhabitants.   35

Letter from Bismarck to William I, 11 October 1863, Heinrich von Sybel, *The Founding of the German Empire by William I*, New York, 1891, vol. IV, pp. 215–18

Questions

1   What does Rechberg mean by the following:
    (i) 'the old ruts ... to the injury of both' 4.5 (i), [lines 6–8]
    (ii) 'This fact gives the answer to the question, which inexplicable
        magic is contained for us in the simple word 'tariff-union' [4.5
        (ii), **lines 7–8]**?
2   What problems exist in Austro–Prussian relations according to Rech-
    berg [**4.5**]? What other problems can be identified?
3   What do Bismarck's marginal comments in **4.5** suggest?
4   How is Napoleon III portrayed in **4.8**?
5   No account of the meeting at Biarritz exists. Why should historians
    therefore be cautious in using Bismarck's account in **4.6**?
6   How else did Bismarck prepare for war with Austria?

4.7   Peace with Austria: the Nickolsberg Memorandum from Bismarck to William I, 24 July 1866

Regarding the negotiations with Austria to find a basis for peace, I
respectfully beg your Majesty to allow me to lay before you the
following considerations:

It seems to me of greatest importance that the present favourable
moment should not be missed. [*Marginal note by William I:* Agreed]
By Your Majesty's declared acceptance *en bloc* of the proposals of His
Majesty the Emperor of the French, the danger of France's taking
sides against Prussia, which by diplomatic pressure could easily turn
into active participation, has been eliminated ... We cannot count on
support from the other great powers for further, or even these,
Prussian demands. Your Majesty has observed in the letters of H.M.
the Emperor of Russia with what alarm he views the Prussian conditions. His Minister, Prince Gortschakow, has also expressed the
wish to know these conditions, both through Your Majesty's
ambassador in St Petersburg and Baron Oubril in Berlin. [*William I:*
Russia's proposal for congress is already evidence of this, for Russia
will use this to oppose preliminaries.] The family connections of the
Russian Imperial house with German dynasties give rise to the fear
that in further negotiations sympathy with them will carry great weight.
In England, public opinion begins to veer towards Your Majesty's
military victories: but the same cannot be said of the government,
and it can only be assumed that it will recognise the *faits accomplis*.

    The double declaration of Austria that it will withdraw from the

German Bund and agree to a reconstruction of it under Prussia's
leadership without Austrian participation, and that it will recognise   25
everything that Your Majesty thinks fit to do in N. Germany, pro-
vides all the essentials that Prussia demands of her. The preservation
of the Kingdom of Saxony is the wish of both Austria and France.
[*William I:* That besides the preservation of the Kingdom of Saxony
its integrity will also be guaranteed, bears very hard on me, as   30
Saxony was the chief instigator of the war and has come out of it
unimpaired]...

If this goal can be assured on this basis by a rapid conclusion of
the preliminaries, then in my humble opinion it would be a political
blunder to put the whole outcome in jeopardy by attempting to wrest   35
from Austria a few more square miles of territory or a few more
millions of war payments, and expose it to the risk of a prolonged
war or negotiations in which foreign intervention could not be
excluded. [*William I:* Agreed, but it depends on how much money or
land can be acquired without risking everything in one throw] ...   40

If your Majesty will give Your consent to this interpretation, I will
have to seek Your Majesty's authority to present to the *Landtag* the
necessary bills for the extension of the boundaries of the kingdom ...
I am very conscious of my responsibility to Your Majesty for the
advice I am called upon to give, and therefore feel the necessity of   45
confirming officially that, even if I dutifully carry out every one of
Your Majesty's conditions in the negotiations, any hindering of a
speedy settlement with Austria by seeking to obtain secondary advantages, will be contrary to my respectful counsel and suggestions.
[*William I:* If in spite of what we apparently have the right to expect   50
of the defeated power it is not possible to demand what the army and
the country have a right to expect, namely heavy indemnities from
Austria as the main enemy or territorial gain to a really visible extent,
without endangering the main object [see above], then the victor will
have to bite into this sour apple at the gates of Vienna and leave it to   55
posterity to judge. Nikolsberg, 25.7.66 William.]

Quoted in H. von Petersdorff et. al. (eds), *Bismarck: Die Gesammelten
Werke*, Berlin, 1923, vol. iv, pp. 79–81

Questions

1   Against what point of view was Bismarck arguing in 4.7? What
arguments does he use to persuade William I?

2   What other thoughts is Bismarck likely to have had which are not mentioned in **4.7**? Why do you think they are not mentioned in **4.7**?
3   William I seems to accept Bismarck's arguments, yet not everybody around him did. What does the last marginal comment by William [**lines 50–56**] tell us about Bismarck's difficulties?
4   With reference to the sources and your wider reading, why did Prussia defeat Austria in the Seven Week War?
5   'The lenient treatment of Austria dulled the inevitable desire for revenge and facilitated the healing of painfully deep wounds.' Discuss.

Germany after 1866

The North German Confederation was established with a superficially liberal constitution which firmly secured Prussian domination. It was very similar to the constitution of 1870 which will be considered later. Within Prussia, Bismarck was riding on the crest of the wave. 'Almost overnight the Bismarck cult was born', comments Otto Pflanze on the events after the defeat of Denmark. This continued after the defeat of Austria.

4.8   The views of historian J. Droysen, from Schleswig-Holstein, on (i) the liberals and (ii) Bismarck. Letters from J. G. Droysen 1863–66. Droysen was a Liberal and a supporter of the Kleindeutschland solution

> (i) Even if, as I believe, the military reorganisation was itself a good thing and in any event cannot be suspended now in view of the great dangers from abroad and in spite of all the many serious shortcomings of the army, that does not make Bismarck etc. any less intolerable. It is nothing short of revolting that this group should use this measure which is correct in itself to cover up its passage by arbitrary force. From the very beginning there has been a group who desire this measure not because it was good but because it was to cloak the way it was to be forced through. I do not know whether this brutality or that of the extreme Left will win the day in the end. In any case the Prussian state and freedom are finished.
>
> **Letter from Droysen to Heinrich von Sybel, 19 October 1863**

(ii) There is no longer any getting away from the fact that Count Bismarck has a rare capacity for statesmanship which it would be unfair to judge according to so-called principles, that is to say, according to pre-conceived and hardened opinions and conclusions drawn from such and such precedents and ideas; whereas what is at 5 stake is to take a step ahead, not merely to see the new possibilities but to realise them ... And this man, glowing coldly, passionately moderate, heedless of friend and foe, of parties and principles, entirely rooted in the facts, in the reality of this state, can act. If the nation had more understanding than indolence, more sincerity than 10 deception, more recognition of its weaknesses and its misery, than comfortable, lazy complacency in its humble and humiliating position, it would thank God that at last a Hercules has arrived to clean out the Augean stables that it has fouled. But many of them, above all our German brothers in the south, go on preferring to roll about 15 in their own filth ... And this is what my friends in Göttingen call profound feeling of the German nation for justice. And I can already see how, when they have succeeded in obstructing what could now be accomplished easily, they will cry spitefully: you see, he couldn't do it either! And yet they ramble on about Germany and German might in 20 every beer hall...

In my estimation these stubborn Swabians, these beery Bavarians, these Catholicised Franks and Alemanni have lost not only their sense of humour but their sense as well. For the first time we have in Germany a free organization without direction of foreign powers, a 25 truly national one. And in the meantime the honourable fragments of the German people exceed the much-scorned dynasties in their silly resistance to the greatest step forward that we have taken in centuries, since 1517 ...

Letter from Droysen to Rudolph Ehmek, 14 October 1866, in W. N. Simon, *Germany in the Age of Bismarck*, 1968, pp. 104–5

4.9 The attitude of the south: an example written by Jakob Venedy from Cologne, a Liberal politician

Prussia was and is dominated by a political orientation that could not and cannot lead to German unity. If this policy, which has found its archetype in Count Bismarck, conquered Germany tomorrow and unified it by force, then even this conquest of all Germany would not lead to German unity. A conquest of Germany by a Prussia that is not ruled in a German spirit would be merely a bare fact that would last until it was superseded by another fact. The unity of Germany must be founded on something beyond the 'majestic thundering of cannon' ... it must be rooted in German respect for law, German popular honour and popular self-government if it is to last ...

The unity of Germany can be realized only by and with the German people, not by a 'Crown' with the help of a party that scorns German law and German nationality. A parliament of the whole German people is the natural bond among all the German peoples. In 1848 the nation was launched in the right direction, and if Prussia, the Prussian 'Crown' had at that time accepted the national constitution and the imperial crown then it would have been legitimate to fight against Austria and the enemies of the nation and the emperor. But the Prussian 'Crown' did not want to accept the 'Crown' of Germany from the hands of the German people ...

Quoted in W. N. Simon, *Germany in the Age of Bismarck,* **1958, p. 124**

4.10   Bismarck's perception of the future, in letters to (i) the Prussian ambassador to Britain, and (ii) his Munich envoy

(i) We perceive our immediate task to be the consolidation of the North German Confederation. We should be afraid to make the performance of this task more difficult for ourselves, and to disturb it by premature attempts to draw south Germany into our political sphere. Force of circumstances will be sufficient to guide the relations between the south German states and Prussia along the right path towards the goal of German unification ...

Letter from Bismarck to the Prussian ambassador of Britain, 14 January 1867, in H. Oncken, *Die Rheinpolitik Kaiser Napoleons III 1863–70,* **1926, vol. II, No. 336, p. 184**

(ii) That German unity could be promoted by actions involving force, I think is self-evident. But there is quite a different question and that has to do with the precipitation of a powerful catastrophe and the responsibility of choosing the time for it. A voluntary intervention in the evolution of history, which is determined by purely subjective factors, results only in the shaking down of unripe fruit, and that German unity is not ripe fruit at this time leaps, in my opinion, to the eye. If the time that lies ahead works in the interest of

unity as much as the period since the accession of Frederick the
Great has done, and particularly the period since 1840, the year in   10
which a national movement was perceptible for the first time since
the war of liberation, then we can look to the future calmly and leave
the rest to our successors. Behind the wordy restlessness with which
people who do not know the trade search after the talisman that will
supposedly produce German unity in a trice, there is generally hid-   15
den a superficial and, in any case, impotent lack of knowledge of real
things and their consequences.

**Letter from Bismarck to his Munich envoy, von Werthern, 26 February
1869, in H. von Petersdorff et al (eds),** *Bismarck: Die Gesammelten
Werke***, Berlin, 1923, vib. 1**

Questions

1 How did Droysen's views [4.8] of Bismarck change between 1862 and
   1866? How can you account for such a marked change of mind?
2 Why is Droysen so contemptible of the southern states?
3 How does Venedy [4.9] support the argument set out in the first
   sentence? Venedy and Droysen were both liberals. Explain how it was
   possible for their view to differ profoundly over the same issue.
4 In what ways and for what reasons did both politicians allude to
   historical events in 4.8 and 4.9?
5 How far do 4.8 and 4.9 help explain Bismarck's attitude towards the
   future of Germany in 4.10?
6 How reliable an indicator of Bismarck's intentions do you regard
   4.10?
7 'Today more than ever before politicians must ask, not what is
   desirable but what is attainable' (J. Miguel, German Liberal, 1866).
   Is it fair to argue that Prussian liberals 'sold out' to Bismarck?
8 What conditions militated against the inclusion of the southern states
   in 1866?

5 The war with France

Bismarck's goal was the unification of Germany under Prussian control. This had already been partially achieved, but even Bismarck was uncertain when the inclusion of the southern states would occur. Nevertheless he always looked for opportunities, with comparatively little success before 1870. The particularism of the southern states and the hostility of France were the principal obstacles. Whilst Bismarck vowed that he would 'never consent to a war that is avoidable, much less seek it,' he was well aware that victory in war against France would overcome them both. War was not his sole aim, but it was one of a variety of possibilities open to him.

This chapter looks at the lead up to the outbreak of the Franco–Prussian War. An important question to consider is how far Bismarck was responsible for the war, and how far it was a product of other factors, such as the policies of the French government. The final section deals with reaction to the war and the nature of the war itself.

Relations with France after the defeat of Austria

The strengthening of Prussia in Germany and the decline of Austria was a potential threat to France who, under Napoleon III, sought expansion to her 'natural frontiers'. It was therefore essential to Napoleon III to check further Prussian expansion. Bismarck perceived that the French would not tolerate Prussian aggrandisement without substantial compensation. He also realised that war was the most effective way of generating nationalist enthusiasm in the southern states, which harboured somewhat paradoxical attitudes towards inclusion in the new Germany.

5.1   The Luxemburg and Limburg Treaty, 11 May 1867

> *Article II* The Grand Duchy of Luxemburg, within the limits determined by the Act annexed to the Treaties of the 19 April 1839, under the Guarantee of the Courts of Great Britain, Austria, France, Prussia and Russia, shall henceforth form a perpetually Neutral State ...

Article III The Grand Duchy of Luxemburg being neutralized, according to the terms of the preceding Article, the maintenance or establishment of fortresses upon its territory becomes without necessity as well as without object.

In consequence, it is agreed by common consent that the City of Luxemburg, considered in time past, in a military point of view, as a federal fortress, shall cease to be a fortified city.

His Majesty the King Grand Duke reserves to himself to maintain in that city the number of troops necessary to provide in it for the maintenance of good order.

Article IV In conformity with the stipulations contained in Articles II and III, His Majesty the King of Prussia declares that his troops actually in garrison in the Fortress of Luxemburg shall receive orders to proceed with the Evacuation of that place immediately after the exchange of the ratifications of the present Treaty...

Article V His Majesty the King Grand Duke ... engages, on his part, to take necessary measures for converting the said fortress into an open city by means of a demolition which His Majesty shall deem sufficient...

E. Hertslet, *The Map of Europe by Treaty*, 1875, vol. 3, pp. 1803–5

5.2

France warns Prussia: 'Now you're big enough. You mustn't get any bigger. I'm telling you this for your own health.'

Cartoon from Punch, 1867

5.3   Napoleon III in conversation with Lord Augustus Loftus, British ambassador to Berlin, 1868

I [Lord Augustus Loftus] had a long conversation with His Imperial Highness on the day after his arrival. It then appeared to me that his attention was mostly, if not entirely, occupied with the present and future of Germany. He disclaimed any identification with the present ministry or policy of France, and frankly said that he was in opposition to the government, and that, consequently, his opinions were purely private and personal. He spoke of the reconstruction of Germany saying that what had been done was not a *fait accompli*, and recognised by France. He did not seem to entertain any hopes, or even a wish, that what had been so far effected could be altered. He even said that the absorption of the smaller northern states was of no importance to France. 'But', observed His Imperial Highness, 'the unification of Germany under Prussia is still in progress. The Zollverein parliament is a step further to the absorption of southern Germany. Where is this to end? What limit is to be placed to the Germany of the future – or, rather, to Prussia?'

'Then again,' said His Imperial Highness, 'if the principle of nationality is carried out – the legitimate grounds for such a policy – what will become of the eight millions of Austro-Germans? Will their turn come next? And how will it be possible for them to avoid being drawn into the same vortex?

'It may be very well to say that Germany is not an aggressive Power, but who can say when she may not become so? And that she may not some day reclaim Alsace and Lorraine, or seek to unite within her boundaries the Russo-German provinces of the Baltic?

'You English have chosen to withdraw yourselves from the political arena of Europe, and this abstention of England from active participation in European politics is a great misfortune for Europe, and will later prove to be a great misfortune for herself.

'There are two points on which England keeps a watchful and jealous eye – namely, Belgium and Constantinople. If any idea is ever mooted which could menace the independence of Belgium, England will immediately raise her voice. If Russia discloses any secret design on Constantinople, there again you raise a cry of alarm. But as regards the charge brought about and in operation in Germany you are apparently apathetic, and foresee no danger likely to affect your interests.

'Let a Germany be constituted, but let its limits be fixed and final,

so that it may not be led to aspire to future aggrandisement; and let
the arrangement concluded be placed under European guarantee.'   40

The Diplomatic Reminiscences of Lord Augustus Loftus, 1862–79, 1894,
vol. 1, pp. 216–20

5.4   Bismarck's view of the Candidature, in a letter to William I

Your Majesty will, I trust, graciously permit me, with my humble
duty to summarize in writing, the motives, which in my modest
opinion, favour the acceptance of the Spanish Crown by His Serene
Highness the Hereditary Prince of Hohenzollern...

I am of the opinion that if the acceptance takes place it will bring   5
both direct and indirect advantages for Prussian and German political
interests and that, in the opposite case, disadvantages and dangers are
to be feared.

Acceptance of the Spanish Royal Crown by a Prince of Your
Majesty's illustrious House would strengthen existing sympathies   10
between two nations which are, by way of exception, in the happy
position of having no conflicting interests because they are not neighbours. Their friendly relations seem capable of considerable development. The Spaniards would feel a sense of gratitude towards
Germany, if she were to rescue them from the state of anarchy into   15
which they – a people predominantly monarchist in sentiment –
threaten to sink for want of a King.

It is desirable for Germany to have on the far side of France a
country on whose sympathy she can rely and with those susceptibili-
ties France would be obliged to reckon ...   20

French peaceableness towards Germany will always wax or wane in
proportion to the dangers of war with her. We have in the long run
to look for the preservation of peace not to the goodwill of France
but to her impression of our power.

The prosperity of Spain and Germany's trade with her would   25
receive a powerful impetus under Hohenzollern rule. If even in
Romania the German dynasty has given a remarkable stimulus to
trade relations between that landlocked country and Germany, it is to
be assumed that in all probability the revival of friendly feelings
towards Germany in Spain with her long coastline would provide   30
new openings there for German trade, once so prosperous...

Letter from Bismarck to William I, 9 March 1870, in *Bismarck: Die
Gesammelte Werke*, vol. VIb, no. 1521, p. 271

Questions

1   Study cartoon **5.2**. What was the cartoonist's attitude towards:
     (i) France   (ii) Prussia?
2   On what grounds were the cartoonist's views based? Were they borne
     out by the Luxemburg affair and in what ways?
3   What parts of the Luxemburg and Limburg Treaty [**5.1**] were
     unsatisfactory to: (i) Prussia   (ii) France?
     Explain.
4   'The Luxemburg affair was the turning point in Bismark's develop-
     ment from a Prussian to a German statesman' (F. Eyck). Discuss.
5   Study the conversation in **5.3**. What are Napoleon III's fears regard-
     ing Germany? Why does he feel France is particularly vulnerable?
6   Bismarck told a British journalist in 1867 that 'there is nothing in our
     attitude to annoy or alarm France'. Does this mean that Napoleon
     III's fears were groundless? Justify your answer fully.

The Spanish Candidature and the outbreak of the Franco–Prussian War

The events surrounding the Spanish Candidature have generated much
controversy amongst historians. In his memoires Bismarck liked to
maintain that he had nothing to do with the affair, the war being a result
of French belligerence. Yet, as historians like Bonnin, writing in 1957,
have shown, he was implicated from the outset. The fundamental
question is why he became involved. Was it to humiliate France? Did he
seek war from the start? Or did his motives evolve with changing
circumstances?

**5.5   Bismarck receives and emends the Ems telegram, 13 July 1870.
The original telegram from the King**

> His Majesty the King writes to me: 'Count Benedetti accosted me on
> the grounds to demand from me, in an ultimately tiresome manner,
> authority for him to telegraph immediately that I would pledge myself
> henceforward never again to give my consent if the Hohenzollerns
> should renew their candidature. I refused him, finally quite earnestly,
> as one dare not and cannot for all time enter into such agreements.
> Naturally I told him I had as yet received no news and, as he had
> been notified about Paris and Madrid earlier than I, he would cer-
> tainly see that my government again had no hand in the matter.'

Since then His Majesty has received a letter from Charles Antony.   10
His Majesty having told Count Benedetti that he was expecting news
from the Prince, with regard to the foregoing demand, has decided, at
the suggestion of Count Eulenberg and myself, not to receive Count
Benedetti again, but merely to have an adjutant tell him that His
Majesty had received confirmation of the news which Benedetti had   15
already had from Paris, and that he had nothing further to say to the
ambassador.

His Majesty leaves it to Your Excellency whether or not Benedetti's
new demand and its refusal should be made known immediately both
to our ambassadors and in the press.   20

Quoted in L. D. Steefel, *Bismarck, the Hohenzollern Candidacy, and the
Origins of the France–German War of 1879*, Harvard, 1962, pp. 257–58

5.6   Bismarck's description of the amendment

Having decided to resign, I invited [Roon] and Moltke to dine with
me alone on the 13th, and communicated to them at table my views
and projects for doing so. Both were greatly depressed ... During our
conversation I was informed that a telegram from Ems ... was being
deciphered. When the copy was handed to me it showed that Abeken   5
had drawn up and signed the telegram at his Majesty's command,
and I read it out to my guests, whose dejection was so great that they
turned away from food and drink. On a repeated examination of the
document I lingered upon the authorization of His Majesty, which
included a command, immediately to communicate Benedetti's fresh   10
demand and its rejection both to our ambassadors and the Press. I
put a few questions to Moltke as to the extent of his confidence in
the state of our preparations, especially as to the time they would still
require in order to meet this sudden risk of war.

[Several] considerations, conscious and unconscious, strengthened   15
my opinion that war could be avoided only at the cost of the honour
of Prussia and of the national confidence in it. Under this conviction
I made use of the royal authorization communicated to me through
Abeken, to publish the contents of the telegram, and in the presence
of my two guests I reduced the telegram by striking out words, but   20
without adding or altering, to the following form: 'After the news of
the renunciation of the hereditary Prince of Hohenzollern had been
officially communicated to the imperial government of France by the

royal government of Spain, the French ambassador at Ems further demanded of his Majesty the King that he would authorize him to telegraph to Paris that his Majesty the King bound himself for all future time never again to give his consent if the Hohenzollerns should renew their candidature. His Majesty the King thereupon decided not to receive the French ambassador again, and sent to tell him through the *aide-de-camp* on duty that his Majesty had nothing further to communicate to the ambassador.' The difference in the effect of the abbreviated text of the Ems telegram as compared with that produced by the original was not the result of stronger words but of the form, which made this announcement appear decisive, while Abeken's version would only have been regarded as a fragment of a negotiation still pending, and to be continued at Berlin.

After I had read out the concentrated edition to my guests, Moltke remarked: 'Now it has a different ring; it sounded before like a parley; now it is like a flourish in answer to a challenge.' ...

Bismarck: The Man and the Statesman, 1899, vol. II, pp. 96–8, 100–2

Questions

1   How does Bismarck attempt to persuade the King of the advantages of acceptance of the Canditature in **5.4**? How convincing are his arguments?

2   'The most interesting thing of this curious document – whose arguments the King refuted energetically and effectively – was what it did not say' (G. Craig). Examine this comment with detailed reference to **5.4**.

3   Account for the feeling of despondancy described at the start of **5.6**.

4   What were Bismarck's motives in editing the telegram [**5.6**]? How does the revised telegram differ from the original [**5.5**]? What impact do you think it was meant to have?

5   Source **5.6**. was written by Bismarck many years after the event. What parts of it should be treated with caution by historians and why?

The outbreak of war

The release of the Ems telegram and the French declaration of war on 19 July produced a variety of reactions. On 25 July, Bismarck cunningly released the demands for compensation made by the French in 1866; he carefully omitted the date. This act had the desired effect upon other Powers.

5.7   The reaction in *The Times*

[This document] may be assumed to have been offered to the Court
of Berlin at the time when the neutralization of Luxemburg had not
been completed, and when the stipulations of the Treaty of Prague
were still seriously debated... Hence the Emperor proposes to admit
and recognize all the acquisitions Prussia made at the end of the war   5
in Bohemia, while the King was to bind himself to facilitate the
acquisition by France of Luxemburg... No opposition was to be
raised on the part of France to a Federal Union of all the south
German states, except Austria... and again the King of Prussia was
invited to bind himself, in case the Emperor should be drawn by   10
circumstances, to throw his troops into Belgium or to conquer it... It
was rejected, but, unless we are misinformed ... the Treaty has been
recently again offered as a condition of peace...

    The revelation of this proposed Treaty sheds a new light on the
Proclamation of the Emperor, and on the petty accusations of the   15
dispute which have been paraded before Europe during the past
fortnight ... M. Ollivier talks of an unusual and insulting Despatch to
all courts of Europe, which no one has even seen. ... Peaceful diplomacy was met with contempt. If this be true, we may ask, who has
made it true? If France be on fire, who has fanned the flames? The   20
Emperor asserts that France did not make war on Germany, whose
independence she respects ... How is the independence of Germany
to be respected simultaneously with the establishment of new guaran-
tees of French security? The simple explanation is to be found in the
interpretation of the word 'Germany' as shall define the German   25
nationality within the bounds of the Rhine. If this be the meaning of
the Emperor, we cannot contemplate it without remembering the
ulterior aims manifested in the draught Treaty.

The Times, 25 July 1870

5.8   Southern support: the Bavarian legislature votes to support the Hohenzollerns, as described by statesman Bernhard von Bülow, 1921–26

At the very beginning of his speech Jörg [leader of the 'Patriots'
Party] had the audacity to persist in declaring that the quarrel
between Prussia and France lay outside the realm of German
integrity and honour. The whole of the present complication had,
he said, originated in the policy of the Prussian ruling House.   5

Full of dignity, calmly and firmly, Count Bray, the Premier, replied to the 'Patriot' Jörg: 'The matter before us is one of keeping or breaking the treaty. We must declare our attitude toward Germany.' The unrestrained applause of the Liberals and government benches resounded when these words were spoken. The premier concluded: 'I have not lived until now merely to renounce my principles, revoke my signature.' After him the Minister of War, the good Baron von Prankh, stood up to speak. Like the Premier before him, he spoke not as a politician, not as a jurist, but only as a soldier, a true Bavarian, an old Bavarian, but also a German. In a manly speech he made a last appeal to the Chamber. 'Let us stand by Germany,' he said, 'otherwise we are dishonoured and lost.' In vain the 'Patriots' Dr Ruhland and Dr Westermayer, prelate and priest of St Peter's, Munich, tried to help Jörg, the Party chief. In their ecclesiastical capacity they were agitators rather than priests. The former protested against thrusting the sons of Bavaria into a sanguinary war with an enemy who had never given personal offence to the Bavarians themselves. Dr Westmayer held the sanctimonious opinion that there was a standpoint in morals where care for the hearth and home took precedence over the duty of helping a menaced neighbour... The Liberal deputies, Fisher, Völk, Edel, Marquardsen, and Barth, drawing attention to the cheers for the Fatherland that could be heard inside the House and came from the crowds outside the Chamber, appealed in fiery words to German patriotism and German honour. The Speaker, Weiss, made a last weak attempt to adjourn the debate because 'pressure' was being brought to bear upon the discussion, but after some irresolution, finally allowed the vote to be taken. Jörg's motion in Committee was defeated by 89 votes to 58, and the government's proposal [i.e. to join in the war] accepted by 101 votes to 47.

Memoirs of Prince von Bülow, 1931–32, vol. IV, pp. 163–65

5.9 A French view of the origins of the Franco–Prussian war, by Emile Ollivier, French Premier at the outbreak of war, writing in later years

In 1866, on the field of Sadowa, Austria not only lost her former preponderance in the Germanic Confederation, but was excluded therefrom. The intervention of France prevented the victory of Prus-

sia from being complete: she was allowed to annex certain territory,
but the states of the south were set outside of her Confederation, and   5
the Main became the artificial boundary between the two sections of
Germany. Thenceforth Bismarck's policy had but one object: to
destroy the boundary and to throw bridges across the Main whereby
the two sections of Germany might be united. With keen and intelligent foresight, he saw that there could be no drawing together of the   10
states of the north and those of the south so long as the gory
memories of 1866 stood between them. A campaign made by them in
common against France seemed to him the only means of wiping out
all trace of these internal dissensions.

For some time he hoped that France would seek an encounter, and   15
would try to recover the preponderance of which the victory of
Sadowa had deprived her; but France perorated, sulked, and did not
stir...

The cause of the conflict between Germany and France was only
one of those 'artificial fatalities', born of the false conceptions or   20
unhealthy ambitions of statesmen, which with lapse of time become
worn out, transformed, and often extinguished...

But there was a man to whom it was important that that artificial
fatality should exist and should end in war...

Napoleon III wanted peace, but with a vacillating will; Bismarck   25
wanted war, with an inflexible will: the inflexible will overcame the
vacillating will. A fresh proof, as that profound thinker Gustave Le
Bon so forcibly says, that 'the faith that raises mountains is named
the will. It is the true creator of things'...

Emile Ollivier, *The Franco–Prussian War and its hidden Causes*, Boston
1912, pp. 13, 400–4

5.10   Bismarck reflects in the 1890s on the origins of the War

I assumed that a united Germany was only a question of time, that
the North German Confederation was only the first step in its solution... I did not doubt that a Franco–German war must take place
before the construction of a united Germany could be realised... I
was at that time pre-occupied with the idea of delaying the outbreak   5
of this war until our fighting strength should be increased...

Bismarck, *Reflections and Reminiscences*, vol. 2, 1898

Questions

1   To what document is *The Times* referring in **5.7, line 1**? What inferences does it draw? How reasonable were these inferences?

2   What arguments are put forward in **5.8.** both in favour and against Bavaria joining Prussia in the war against France? How do you account for the strength of feeling in favour of joining Prussia, considering the strength of separatist feeling which had existed in the south, especially since 1866?

3   To what does Ollivier attribute the outbreak of war [**5.9**]? How reasonable is this argument?.

4   **5.10** was written by Bismarck in the 1890s. Is it a more accurate explanation for the outbreak of war than Ollivier's? Explain your answer fully. How reliable do you think **5.10** is as a source of evidence, and why?

5   What were the most important causes of the Franco–Prussian war? Why did the southern states become involved?

The War

The Prussian Army fared much better that the French in all aspects of the campaign. Better led, equipped and more experienced, it soon defeated the French at Sedan on 2 September, contrary to expectation outside Germany. Calls for annexation led to a continuation of the war, ending with the shelling of Paris in January 1871.

5.11   Bismarck's attitude towards the shelling of Paris, as recalled by Heinrich Abeken, a close associate of Bismarck

The idea of Bismarck opposing the bombardment of Paris because of its works of art or the splendours of Paris itself, is incredibly ridiculous. I think nothing in Paris would give him a transient desire to spare it, if he considered the bombardment right from a political and military point of view. As there are so few signs of the Parisians coming to reason, it will be right and necessary to bombard it. We cannot wish the people to be brought to their sense by hunger; the effect of that would be frightful, so it will be far better for them to be bombarded than forced by hunger to submit.

Bismarck's Pen, The Life of Heinrich Abeken, edited from his letters and journals by his wife, London, 1911, pp. 281–82

5.12

'Paris cooked in her own fat', French cartoon, 1871

Questions

1   In what ways do sources **5.11** and **5.12** agree? How was it possible for a French and a German commentator to come to similar conclusions on this issue? What do you infer from this paradox?

2   Here are five interpretations that could be placed upon the events leading up to the outbreak of the Franco–Prussian War:
    (i) Bismarck did not want war at any stage
    (ii) Bismarck sought to humiliate France with the Candidature and France could either back down or go to war. Either way, Prussia would gain
    (iii) Bismarck was forced into a war by a bellicose France
    (iv) Bismarck was forced into a war by a bellicose French and German popular nationalism
    (v) Bismarck sought war with France all along
    Using the documents in this chapter and your broader knowledge of the period, say which of the above you agree with and why. If you have your own interpretation, explain it fully.

3   'What should be noted is that whereas the Austro–Prussian clash had an air of fatality about it, the necessity for a war between the North German Confederation and France was much less. The former led to a quick reconciliation; the latter to enduring enmity' (Waller). Discuss.

6 Unification

The unexpectedly rapid and spectacular defeat of France generated a wave of nationalist excitement across Germany, including the south, where governments consented to inclusion in the new Reich. In this final chapter we will firstly analyse the nature of German unification in 1870–71, and especially the attitude of the south. We will then look at a wide variety of contemporary comments, inside and beyond Germany, concerning the prospects for the new Reich.

The nature of unification

The inclusion of the southern states was not a straightforward affair for Bismarck. Despite the nationalist fervour inspired by the Franco–Prussian War, there were grave doubts amongst many southern politicians that inclusion in the Reich would inevitably lead to an erosion of their sovereignty.

6.1 Arguments of the southern states in favour of unification: a speech by Prince Hohenlohe to the Upper House in Bavaria in 1870

It seems to me that two facts, above all others, have tended to guide German policy into new paths, to modify the position of Bavaria, as it has developed during recent centuries, and to unite the country more closely to Germany.

One of these facts is the awakened spirit of nationalism throughout the German people, and the other is the changed position of the German Great Powers. When Bavaria became a kingdom in 1806 she reached the highest point of that policy which I have styled isolation, and which found its explanation, if not justification, in the general condition of the German Empire and the absence of any national feelings. Bavaria had, formally at least, attained full sovereignty. Yet a few years afterwards the kingdom surrendered important rights in favour of the German Confederation, and the deciding motive in this case was respect for the growing sense of nationality throughout the German people. When the war of liberation had begun, it was impossible to continue the policy of the Rhine Federation. In the

year 1866, after the dissolution of the German Federation, when
Bavaria for the second time secured a doubtful freedom to determine
her own course, the kingdom immediately hastened to sacrifice the
independence she has secured in the convention of 22 August, appar-   20
ently guided by the idea that German nationalism would make the
pursuit of any other policy impossible except that which was
expressed in the convention. You also, my lords, were witness of a
similar turning point in Bavarian history in the autumn of 1867,
when the acceptance or refusal of the convention therewith connected   25
came before you for discussion.

The majority of you at that time could not decide to secure that
economic isolation of Bavaria which would necessarily have resulted
in political isolation. After serious doubts, you made your determi-
nation and voted as you did, because a non-German policy was no   30
longer possible in a German state. When in the summer of this year
the decisive moment approached and it seemed possible for the last
time to enter upon a course which would have replaced Bavaria in the
position of 1806, you resisted the temptations which one party placed
before the Bavarian people and which are rightly termed unpatriotic.   35
You rejected that neutrality which would have led to an alliance with
France. At that time a political opponent cried to me: 'Now the
German Empire is complete.' The prophecy has been fulfilled, not, as
a previous speaker has observed, because military alliance necessarily
implies subordination to the power of the stronger ally; it has been   40
fulfilled because German nationalism has become a power in this war
and a force to which the preference for long-standing institutions
must give way, and before which the antipathetic tendencies of the
German races have disappeared.

Memoirs of Prince Chlodwig of Hohenlohe-Schillingsfurst, New York,
1906, vol. 2, pp. 34–38

6.2   Arguments of the southern states against unification: article by Moritz von Mohl, a politician in Württemberg

What the so-called German question has now become might have
been foreseen at the outbreak of war by anyone who had followed the
course of things since the year 1866 with keen observation or was
acquainted with the efforts of the party that has adopted this question
as its own ...   5
One may be of the opinion that it would be better if Germany

were one single state. We do not share this opinion. On the contrary, we think that the total amount of culture, morality, and prosperity, the mass of civilising and humanising institutions (such as universities, art and professional schools), the closely woven net of communications and so many other advantages which Germany has over France and over other great empires, have their origin in the number of centres from which they may take their beginning and in the mutual composition of the individual German states. It is precisely south Germany and Saxony that are very significant evidence of this. No right-thinking person will deny that intellectual and political freedom would have had a better home in a many-membered Germany than it has ever found in a unitary monarchy.

The situation with which we are confronted is to be rejected absolutely. It is that of lands subject to one great state, the *capitus diminutio* of submitting to a ruling people. *This is* the character which would be imprinted on our states, if they entered the North German Confederation. It will be no different and no better for the fact that the varied and noble north-German states will have preceded this situation by their submission after the events of 1866.

The North German Confederation is only a federation in name. In its real life it is an empire in which a number of vassal states have subjected themselves to the King, the government, and the representative assembly of one great state. The vassal states receive the law from the master state. Their position is all the worse because their people have to bear tax burdens imposed both by the ruling state and by the subject governments, without enjoying any substantial influence over the former nor being at home masters in their own house. Nothing would be changed in all this by entry of the south German states into the North German Confederation as can easily be mathematically proved and as their unfavourable position in the Customs Parliament already adequately shows.

Moritz von Mohl, *Für die Erhaltung der Süddeutschen Staaten*, Stuttgart, 1870, p. 4

6.3   King Ludwig II of Bavaria invites William I to accept the Imperial Crown

After the adhesion of southern Germany to the German constitutional Alliance the Presidential rights vested in your Majesty will

extend over all German States. In consenting to those rights being
vested in a single hand I have been influenced by the conviction that
the interests of the whole German Fatherland and its allied Sover- 5
eigns will be effectually promoted by this arrangement. I trust that
the rights constitutionally possessed by the President of the Confe-
deracy will, by the restoration of the German Empire and the
German Imperial dignity, be recognised as rights exercised by your
Majesty in the name of the entire Fatherland, and by virtue of the 10
agreement effected between its Princes. I have therefore proposed to
the German Sovereigns, conjointly with myself, to suggest to your
Majesty that the possession of the Presidential Rights of the Confe-
deracy be coupled with the Imperial title.

Letter to William I from King Ludwig II, *The Times*, 7 December 1870

6.4 The Constitution of the German Empire (extracts)

Article 5 The Imperial legislative power shall be exercised by the
Bundesrat and the *Reichstag*. The agreement of the majority votes of
both bodies is necessary and sufficient for an imperial statute.

Article 6 The Bundesrat is composed of the representatives of the
members of the Federation, and the voting procedure shall be as 5
follows: Prussia – 17 votes; Bavaria – 6 ... Total 58 votes ... all
delegations must cast their votes as a unit.

Article 7 The Bundesrat shall decide upon: proposals made by the
Reichstag and decisions made by it ...

Article 8 The Bundesrat shall organise from its membership per- 10
manent committees for (1) the Army and its citadels (2) the Navy ...
(6) the judiciary ...

Article 11 The Presiding Officer of the Federation shall be the
King of Prussia, who shall bear the name of German Emperor. The
Emperor shall represent the Empire ... to declare war and conclude 15
peace ... to enter alliances and other treaties with foreign states.

Article 15 The presiding chair in the Bundesrat and the conduct of
business appertain to the Imperial Chancellor, who is appointed by
the Emperor...

Article 20 The Reichstag shall proceed from universal and direct 20
elections with secret voting ...

Article 24 For the dissolution of the Reichstag ... a resolution of the Bundesrat with the concurrence of the Emperor is required...

Article 78 Amendments of the Constitution are made by legislation. They shall be considered rejected if they have fourteen votes against them.

Quoted in J. Hohlfield, ed., *Dokumente der Deutschen Politik und Geschichte*, vol. 1, pp. 201–27 passim

Questions

1   What arguments are used in documents **6.1** and **6.2** to support or oppose the inclusion of the southern states in the rest of Germany? Analyse the strength of each argument.

2   How do Hohenlohe and von Mohl [**6.1 and 6.2**] interpret the events of 1866? Which was the more realistic appraisal?

3   Study the letter **6.3**. Comment on:
  (i) the fact that it was written by Ludwig II
  (ii) the phrase 'by virtue of the agreement effected between its Princes...' [**lines 10–11**]

4   What parts of document **6.4** would be most objectionable to the author of **6.2**? Explain fully.

5   Study the extracts in **6.4**. Comment on:
  (i) the title 'German Emperor' [**line 14**]
  (ii) Article 20

6   Böhme states that 'Ludwig of Bavaria [said that] after 1864 there was 'no other choice'. Compelled by powerful interest they were forced to seek a connection with Prussia.' What evidence do documents **6.1–6.4** provide about those 'powerful interests'?

Comment outside Germany

Many problems confronted the new Germany and in a sense it was little more than a wartime coalition. It was to remain united until 1945 and legislation was rapidly passed after 1871 to reinforce unification; for example, a national bank was set up. Yet the importance of the events of 1870–71 was not missed in Germany and beyond. The following extracts demonstrate a number of different reactions to unification.

6.5   Preliminary peace treaty between Germany and France, 26 February 1871 (extracts). This was later expanded into the Treaty of Frankfurt

1 France renounces in favour of the German Empire all her rights and titles over the territories situated on the East of the frontier hereafter described ... The German Empire shall possess these territories in perpetuity in all sovereignty and property... The frontier, such as it has been described, is marked in green on two identical   5
copies of the map of the territory forming the Government of Alsace...

2 France shall pay His Majesty the Emperor of Germany the sum of 5 milliards francs. The payment of at least 1,000,000,000 francs shall be effected within the year 1871, and the whole of the remainder of   10
the debt in the space of three years, dating from the ratification of the present treaty.

3 The evacuation of the French territory occupied by German troops shall begin the ratification of the present treaty by the National Assembly sitting at Bordeaux. Immediately after that ratification, the   15
German troops shall quit the interior of Paris, as well as the forts on the left bank of the Seine and within the shortest possible delay ... they shall entirely evacuate the *Departments* as far as the left bank of the Seine ... The garrison of Paris is excepted from this disposition, the number of which shall not exceed 40,000 men, and the garrisons   20
indispensably necessary for the safety of the strongholds.
   The evacuation of the *Departments* between the right bank of the Seine and the eastern frontier by German troops shall take place gradually after the ratification of the Definitive Treaty of Peace and the payment of the first 500,000,000 of the contribution stipulated by   25
Article 2 ...

Quoted in E. Hertslet, *The Map of Europe by Treaty*, London 1875, vol. III, pp. 1912–17

6.6

L'EXÉCUTIF

French cartoon showing Favre and Thiers co-operating with the German demands, 1871

6.7   Comment in *The Times*

Two causes make the new Power vigorous and formidable, and they are both the product of the present age. One is the enthusiasm for German nationalism which was generated by the cruel domination of the First Napoleon and has been gaining power ever since, until it has conquered every enemy at home and abroad; the other is the extrusion from the German system of foreign elements, nothing more than a part of Poland remaining, and this being in process of assimilation. The contrast between the new and the old condition is obvious. Within living memory German nationality was utterly dead, and up to 1866 the country was linked with foreign and hostile communities. In 1871 Germany starts independent, ardently patriotic, almost purely national. She is about to have the most powerful instrument of unity, a great popular Assembly, an institution which seems in these days to have a more strongly centralizing influence than any despot can command. The Parliament in which Germany will be represented has not yet been constituted, but if there be anything safe in political prediction it is that this Parliament will

reflect the instincts and impulses which have welded the nation into
one. The Hohenzollerns must prove very different from their traditional character if they neglect to make the best use of so potent an   20
ally. There will be, we think, an inevitable tendency in the Federal
Legislature and Administration to break down the independent auth-
orities which the Minor States have reserved for themselves or have
been suffered by Prussia to retain. We do not expect that the Federal
Representatives will be enthusiastic for the Imperial House; but their   25
certain instinct will be to make Germany one and homogeneous, and
this will necessitate the concentration of even more and more authority in the Imperial hands; the respective armies over which the
Sovereigns have reserved to themselves considerable power, at least in
time of peace, will be gradually fused, it will be found that material   30
improvements can be much more efficiently made by a central
administration; a common legal system, a common judicature will be
demanded, and with each change the authority of Berlin will be
increased, while the Sovereigns of Munich and Stuttgart will tend to
become powerless though honourable Dignitaries of the State. Many   35
people, even among the most patriotic of Germany itself, will feel a
sentimental regret at this change. and sigh after the vanishing independence of the ancient Houses and their pleasant little capitals. But
this will be only the common lot. With us Edinburgh and Dublin had
more of the metropolis about them a century ago than now.   40

The Times, 20 January 1871

6.8   Fear of militarism, as expressed by the Norwegian dramatist, Henrik Ibsen

Then think of our own day's heroes,
Of these Blumenthals and Fritzes,
Of the Herren Generale
Number this and number that!
Under Prussia's ghastly colours –   5
Sorrow's clout of black and white –
Ne'er burst forth achievement's larvae
As the butterfly of song.
They perhaps their silk may spin
For a time, but they die therein.   10

Just in victory lies defeat;
Prussia's sword proves Prussia's scourge.
Ne'er poetic inspiration
Springs from problems that they solve.
Deeds win no response in song,   15
If people noble, free,
Beauty-loving, are transformed
Into staff-machinery –
Bristling with the dirks of cunning
From the time that Herr von Moltke   20
Murdered battle's poetry.

So demonic is the power
That received our world to rule:
And the Sphinx, her wisdom guarding,
When her riddle's solved, is slain.   25
Cipher-victories are doomed.
Soon the moment's blast will veer;
Like a storm on desert-plain
It will fell the false god's race.
Bismarck and the other old ones   30
Will, like Memnon's column-stumps,
Stiff on sage-chair be sitting
Songless to the morning sun.

Printed in T. Hamerow, *The Age of Bismarck*, pp. 139–40

Questions

1   Explain the cartoon 6.6 by detailed reference to document 6.5. Was the intensity of feeling in this cartoon a genuine reflection of French public opinion?

2   How did Bismarck's treatment of France differ from the treatment given to Austria in 1866? How do you account for this difference?

3   What role does 6.7 predict for Parliament in the new Germany? Is it borne out by the extracts in 6.5?

4   What is the attitude of *The Times* [6.7] towards German unification? Explain.

5   Explain Ibsen's concern [6.8] that 'Just in victory lies defeat' [**line 11**].

6 Compare **6.8** with source **6.2**. Explain their similarities and differences.
7 With reference to the sources and your wider reading, what were the most important consequences for Europe of German unification?
8 How important a role did the other great powers in Europe play in German unification?

Comment within Germany

6.9 Bismarck on the completeness of unification, in conversation with the British ambassador, Lord Odo Russell, between 1871 and 1874

In the first instance he [Bismarck] wished to solicit my co-operation in contradicting culumny. It had been reported to him that the Queen of Holland who, for incomprehensible reasons of her own was a bitter enemy of Prussia and of German unity, had succeeded during her frequent visits to England in propagating the idea that Prussia   5
sought to annex the Netherlands with a view to acquiring colonies and a fleet for Germany.

He neither desired colonies or fleets for Germany. Colonies in his opinion would only be a cause of weakness, because colonies could only be defended by powerful fleets, and Germany's geographical   10
position did not necessitate her development into a first class maritime power. A fleet was sufficient for Germany that could cope with fleets like those of Austria, Egypt, Holland, and perhaps Italy, scarcely with that of Russia, but it could not be a German interest so long as she had no colonies to rival maritime powers like England,   15
America, or France. Many colonies had been offered to him, he had rejected them and wished only for coaling stations acquired by treaty from other nations.

Germany was not large enough and strong enough in his opinion, and even the Emperor William's insatiable desire for more territory   20
had not led him to covet the possession of the Netherlands.

He had had trouble and vexation enough to combat the Emperor's desire to annex the German provinces of Austria, the population of which certainly desired to form part of the great German family, but that desire he would oppose as long as he was in power, because he   25
preferred the alliance and friendship of Austria to the annexation of provinces that would add nothing to the strength and security of

Germany and the loss of which would lessen the value of Austria as an ally.

The Swiss, for instance, were a German-speaking nation, but Switzerland was of greater value as an independent friendly neighbour to Germany than as a province of the German Empire.

After the Danish War the Emperor had not spoken to him for a week so displeased was His Majesty with him for not having annexed a larger portion of Denmark. In his opinion Germany had too many Danish-speaking subjects and he would willingly pay out of his own pocket to rid Germany of them, but public opinion would not yet allow a German minister to give up any portion of territory so recently acquired. In like manner he held that Germany had too many Polish subjects, but how to deal with them was a question which must depend on the success of the measures now under discussion for the neutralization of the anti-national Roman Catholic element in the new Empire. It was now evident that the strength of Germany was in the Protestant north, her weakness in the Catholic south.

Paul Knapland ed., *Letters from the Berlin Embassy, 1880–85*, Washington, DC, 1944, pp. 87–89

6.10   The Swiss historian, Jacob Burckhardt, foresees another problem: letters to a friend, Friedrich von Preen, 1872

As far as military affairs are concerned, I have no doubt that I shall see you gradually and cautiously circling round until you steer towards my view of the origin of the last war. In the meantime does it not sound as if it had been deliberately intended and willed?...

I am not unreasonable. Bismarck has only taken into his own hands what would have happened anyhow with the passage of time, but without his aid and against his interests. He saw that the growing democratic–socialist wave would somehow provoke a state of absolute power, whether through the Democrats themselves or through the governments. So he spoke: *'ipse faciam'* – and waged the three wars of 1864, 1866 and 1870.

We are, however, only at the beginning. Is it not true that all our action so far is advised because it is agreeable, dilettant, and fanciful in an increasingly laughable contrast to the high purposefulness, thought out in all its detail, of the military system? This must now set the pattern for all existence. For you, honoured friend, it is now

most interesting to observe how the political and administrative
machine is reorganized on military lines; for me, how the school and
educational system etc., is treated. The workers will fare in the most
surprising way. I have an inkling, which at present looks like com-   20
plete folly, and yet it will not entirely leave me, that the military state
must become a great manufacturer. Those agglomerations of people
in the greater workshops cannot remain eternally the victims of their
need and their greed. A fixed and superintended mass of misery,
graded and in uniform, which begins and ends every day at the beat   25
of a drum, that is what logically must come about...

Certainly, everything is apparently quiet in politics. But our
Berlin masters are, I believe, full of anxiety, not on account of foreign
countries but on account of their basically false position in face of the
nation. The external apparatus of so-called freedom has been allowed   30
to come into existence, but they are secretly resolved to act for all
times according to their own will – not that I would deem absolute
government as especial misfortune as compared with the consequences of universal suffrage. I have become extremely cool about
such things. But I fear a new war as the only diversion from internal   35
complexities ...

Quoted in H. Böhme, *The Foundation of the German Empire*, Oxford,
1971, pp. 35–39

6.11   Friedrich Nietzsche, the philosopher, writing in 1873 on German culture and the victory of 1871

Public opinion in Germany seems almost to forbid any discussion of
the evil and dangerous consequences of war, especially of a victorious
war ... Nevertheless, it must be said; a great victory is a great danger.
Human nature finds it harder to bear than a defeat; it seems easier,
paradoxically, to attain such a victory than to behave in such a way   5
that it does not turn into a heavy defeat. Of all the evil consequences
following in the wake of the recent war against France the worst,
perhaps, is a ... general error: the error of public opinion and of all
those who air their opinions in public to the effect, that German
culture also won a victory in that conflict and therefore deserves to be   10
decorated with the laurels appropriate to such extraordinary events
and successes. This delusion is highly pernicious: not at all because it
is a delusion – for some errors are most salutary and beneficial – but
rather because it is capable of converting our victory into a complete

defeat: the defeat, even the death of German culture for the benefit
of the 'German Empire'.

The assertion [that German culture defeated France] appears quite
incomprehensible. It is precisely in the wider knowledge of German
officers, in the better instruction of the German troops, in the more
scientific conduct of the war that all impartial observers and even the
French themselves saw the decisive advantage. But in what sense can
the victory be said to have been that of German education as distinct
from German proficiency? In no sense: for the moral qualities of
stricter discipline and steadier obedience have nothing to do with
education ...

Culture is above all unity of artistic style in all the manifestations
of a people's life. But to have learned and to know a great deal is
neither a means to culture nor a sign if it could, if necessary, quite
easily coexist with the opposite of culture, barbarism: that is, absence
of style or chaotic mixtures of all styles.

But such a chaotic mixture is characteristic of this country today;
and it is a serious problem how Germans, despite all the information
at their disposal, can possibly not notice this and can even heartily
rejoice in their present 'culture'... This sort of 'culture', which is
really nothing but a phlegmatic insensitivity to all culture, cannot be
used to defeat enemies, least of all those who, like the French, have a
genuine and productive culture, no matter of what quality, and whom
we have imitated in everything, mostly without any skill.

N. Simon, *Germany in The Age of Bismarck*, 1958, pp. 155–57

6.12   Adolf Hitler writing in 1924

Today it seems to me providential that Fate should have chosen
Braunau-am-Inn as my birthplace. For this little town lies on the
boundary between two German states which we of the younger
generation at least have made it our life's work to reunite by every
means at our disposal.

German-Austria must return to the great German mother country,
and not because of any economic considerations. No, and again no:
even if such a union were unimportant from an economic point of
view; yes, even if it were harmful, it must nevertheless take place.
One blood demands one Reich. Never will the German nation possess
the moral right to engage in colonial politics until, at least, it

embraces its own sons within a single state. Only when the Reich borders include the very last German, but can no longer guarantee his daily bread, will the moral right to acquire foreign soil arise from the distress of our own people. Their sword will become our plough, 15 and from the tears of war the daily bread of future generations will grow. And so this little city on the border seems to me the symbol of a great mission.

Adolf Hitler, *Mein Kampf*, 1924

Questions

1   With reference to document **6.9**, explain Bismarck's attitude towards:
   (i) colonies
   (ii) the Kleindeutsch solution of German unification
2   To what extent do you think Bismarck is:
   (i) telling the truth
   (ii) distorting the truth?
   How do you account for this?
3   How far was Burckhardt **[6.10]** justified in saying that:
   (i) 'He saw that the growing democratic–socialist wave would some-
       how provoke a state of absolute power' **[lines 7–9]**
   (ii) 'I fear a new war as the only diversion from internal complexi-
       ties' **[lines 35–36]**?
       Did later events bear him out?
4   How does Nietzsche attack the argument that 'German culture also
   won a victory in that conflict' **[6.11, lines 9–10]**?
5   In **6.12**, what does Hitler mean by:
   (i) 'Today it seems to me providential that Fate should have chosen
       Branau-am-Inn as my birthplace' **[lines 1–2]**
   (ii) 'One blood demands one Reich' **[line 10]**?
6   What can you infer from **6.12** about the legacy of 1871?
   Explain.
7   'The founding of the German Empire ... represented the triumph of
   the mailed fist over the libertarian principle in the life of Central
   Europe' (T. S. Hamerow). Discuss.

Glossary

Allgemeine Deutscher Burschenschaften   Universal German Student Association

autocracy   absolute government by an individual with unrestricted authority

Bund   Confederation. The German Confederation was established in 1815 and lasted until 1866

Bundesrat   Upper House in the North German Confederation and later in the German Empire

Burschenschaften   Liberal and nationalist student societies at German universities

Diet   Assembly. The Diet was the legislative assembly of the German Confederation. It met at Frankfurt

ell   a measure of cloth of $1\frac{1}{4}$ yards

Groschen   German currency denomination

Grossdeutschland   Greater Germany, i.e. including Austria

Junker   East Prussian landowners who dominated the army and the bureaucracy

Kleindeutschland   Little Germany, i.e. excluding Austria

Landtag   Prussian assembly

Landwehr   Prussian reserve army

liberalism   political belief which places stress on freedom, the rights of the individual, and on representative government. Liberals varied a great deal in their degree of radicalism

nationalism   belief in the supremacy of one's own nation

Nationalverein   National Union. A national league of liberals, established in Germany in 1859 to promote German unification under Prussian domination. It was comprised mainly of professional people

particularism   emphasis of smaller states on their independence within a larger grouping

Progressive Party   left-wing liberal political party

protectionism   the use of tariffs to protect a country's industry

realpolitik   realistic politics; politics governed by what is attainable rather than by morality

Reichstag   Lower House in the North German Confederation and later in the German Empire

tariff   list of duties imposed on imported goods

Thaler   German currency denomination. One Thaler equals thirty groschen

Zollverein   German Customs Union, established in 1834

Index

Acknowledgements

The author and publisher are grateful to the following for permission to reproduce illustrations and extracts:
1.2, 1.3, 1.4, 1.7, 1.10, 1.12, 1.14, 2.7, 2.11, 3.1 L. Snyder, *Documents of German History*, © 1958 by Rutgers, The State University, reprinted by permission of Rutgers University Press; 1.11, 2.3(i), 3.4, The Fontana Economic History of Europe, vol. 4, *The Emergence of Industrial Societies*, Professor C. M. Cipolla, Collins Publishers: 1.13 G. de Sauvigny, *Metternich and his Times*, 1962, Darton, Longman and Todd; 2.10 F. Eyck, *The Frankfurt Parliament 1848–49*, 1968, Macmillan; 2.13 Karl Marx, *Revolution and Counter Revolution*, (1871), Unwin Hyman; 3.2, 3.3, translated by Agatha Ramm, 6.10 H. Böhme, *The Foundation of the German Empire*, 1971, Oxford University Press; 3.10 Reprinted from *The Social and Political Conflict in Prussia 1858–64*, by Eugene N. Anderson, by permission of Nebraska Press. Copyright 1954 by the University of Nebraska Press; 4.7 W. N. Medlicott and D. K. Coveney (Eds.) *Bismarck and Europe*, 1971, Edward Arnold; 4.8, 4.9, 6.11 W. N. Simon, *Germany in the Age of Bismarck*, 1968, Unwin Hyman; 5.5 L. D. Steefel, *Bismarck, The Hohenzollern Candidacy, and The Origins of the Franco-German War of 1879*, 1962, Harvard University Press; 6.4, 6.12 Adolph Hitler, *Mein Kampf*, Century Hutchinson Limited

Illustrations   1.5 Sachsische Landesbibliothek, Dresden; 1.6 Ullstein Bilderdienst; 2.5 and 3.9 Bildarchiv Preussischer Kulturbesitz; 4.4 BBC Hulton Picture Library; 5.12 Mansell Collection; 6.6 Roger-Viollet

Every effort has been made to reach copyright holders; the publishers would be pleased to hear from anyone whose rights they have unwittingly infringed.

The author would like to express his gratitude to Stephanie Boyd and Richard Brown for their unflagging help and encouragement.

Glossary   Words printed in *italic* are explained in the Glossary on page 106.

Cover illustration   Bismarck and Napoleon III on the morning after the Surrender of the French Army at Sedan; Hulton–Deutsch Collection

Maps by Reg Piggott